FREEDOM FROM ANXIETY

By Hayley Austin

To Pam

feel the fear and do it anyway
you are amazing.
Love Hails
xxx

First published in May 2019

Book cover design by www.uncaged.online
Published by Uncaged

A catalogue record for this book is available from the British Library.

Paperback ISBN: 978-1-5272-4133-6

I dedicate this book to anyone stuck, stressed and perhaps feeling lost, lacking a sense of purpose and achievement. For everyone and anyone who suffers from anxieties.

Thank you to my husband Mark Austin for always believing in me and being my biggest champion, my knight in shining armour. For allowing me to be me, and for his continued support. My son Jacob Austin for being my biggest challenge to date - becoming a mum - and for bringing me immense joy, purpose and happiness.

My mum Ruth Hughes for giving me life and believing in me without judgement. Our relationship has grown from strength to strength after our revelatory honest and open talks.

To all the clients I have helped - past and present - and to my friends who have great belief in me.

It's never too late to discover who you are and what your purpose is. To get to the bottom of your anxieties and how to overcome them.

This book is to educate and give you the tools to overcome anxiety and to become the best version of YOU.

Foreword by Mark Shields - Founder the Life Practice Academy - aka The CAM Coach

The Birth of Mrs Powers

My senses all came alive at the same time, the hairs on my back stood up, and every sense I owned began to take notice in the scene developing in front of me. It felt like I had awoken from a dream in the middle of the night. Sounds dramatic, doesn't it?! Not only was it dramatic but also unprecedented, as I had never seen anything quite like this before. In my world, something extraordinary was developing right in front of my eyes.

Ok, let me rewind a little to explain the gravity of the situation and set the scene. I was sitting playing the role of a client in the final assessment of one of our first students to graduate from our Life Practice Academy. It was May 2018. I had been training and assessing students since 2005 but had never seen anything like this before.

Hayley Austin - or Mrs Powers as I subsequently named her - was taking me through a 3-hour assessment. During these 3 hours, Hayley skilfully demonstrated life-changing techniques pitch perfect. It was the best 3-hour assessment I had ever seen in 15 years. It was incredible. She demonstrated skills both confidently and competently, skills that would take most people years to get to this standard, if at all. To top it all for Hayley, this was just day one.

There was something incredibly special about this student and as I was soon to learn this was only the beginning.

The next sign that Mrs Powers was going to be an extraordinary coach didn't take long to appear. A few days later Dr Richard Wain, the principal at our course accreditation body (the ACCPH), wrote to me privately.

Due to Hayley's incredible assessment performance and the quality of her work he'd decided to upgrade her final diploma from a level 4 to a level 5. This was now the second first for me. Hayley Austin had blown me away, and I suspected there was more to come. I wasn't wrong.

For all coaches in private practice reading this you will all understand it takes a full 12 months to set up and sustain a successful private coaching practice. Well, this was the third time Hayley blazed a trail through the norm of other newly qualified coaches. She got herself on a local radio show and within weeks had been signed up by a local charity with a mission of helping others.

On her journey home from the radio show Hayley was on fire with enthusiasm and excitement. Mrs Powers had arrived and was here to stay. Hayley was soon changing lives daily facilitating over 64 coaching sessions per month. This in itself is incredible as most new coaches would be working with a handful of clients per month at this early stage.

She was facilitating incredible change with people, curing life-long fears and phobias, and achieving incredible results with clients who'd battled overwhelming anxiety and depression for years, regularly sharing her clients' messages of thanks and gratitude with me.

To summarise, Hayley Austin is without a doubt the most promising student I have ever trained. She is performing and achieving more success than any other student I have ever worked with.

Her book is an incredible read and focuses on a topic that is now very prevalent in society today. Anxiety and fear. We all suffer from anxiety at some point in our lives, and Hayley's book highlights key strategies to take anxiety on and win.

Our mission as a training school is 'to create a positive impact in the world by helping create as many life coaches as possible.' I know for sure the world will be a much more positive place now that Hayley Austin - author, coach and educator AKA Mrs Powers - is in it.

I am proud to have trained her, proud to have been part of her journey and now proud of the trail she is blazing in the world of transformational change coaching.

Mark Shields - The CAM Coach

Contents

Introduction

Anxiety disorders affect 40 million adults in the United States with 85% of adults in a 2018 study experiencing regular bouts of stress in the UK. Stress and anxiety are starting to affect people from a much younger age, with more children than ever on medication or being treated for disordered eating or self-harm. Co-dependence, addiction and uncontrollable anger as well as dis-ease are just some of the ways that our stress and anxiety manifest. The truth is, stress affects us all, whether we're experiencing it directly or indirectly in our environment.

Stress can be a good thing. As you will find in chapter one when we look at stress and anxiety in more depth, stress serves a purpose. However, with the pressure and demands of modern living and a cultural addiction to busy-ness, many of us are living in a chronic state of stress which has a debilitating impact on our wellbeing. The response to short-term stress - our 'fight-or-flight' mode - alerts us to danger and triggers us to respond quickly. Once the threat passes, our system returns to its normal state. When stress becomes chronic, we find ourselves in a prolonged vigilant and reactive state which can lead to digestive issues, a weakened immune system, and burnout, amongst other physical and mental health issues. We become more reactive to people and situations, or we often adopt unhealthy or unwanted behaviours, e.g. excess alcohol consumption or binge eating, as coping mechanisms to self-medicate and deal with our stress.

Our system can become overloaded with excess sensory input from our environment; the more stressed we feel, the more sensitive our senses become, and so our stress response is triggered some more. In a heightened state, we can become all-consumed by our thoughts, our worries escalating into feelings of anxiety, especially when there is no real threat or danger. Before we know it, we can spiral downwards, and what started as a natural and healthy stress response, soon feels like a deep hole that we struggle to get out of. This was certainly my experience.

I was crippled with anxiety to the point that I was too afraid to go out. On the occasions that I did, I'd be looking over my shoulder in fear that someone would hurl abuse at me or attack me, or I'd have to pull over in my car as the first signs of a panic attack started to bubble to the surface. You may say these fears were irrational and completely unfounded, and indeed to anyone on the outside they certainly looked that way. But to me they were real. It was my reality. If someone had told me back then that one day, I'd have a flourishing coaching practice helping others through anxiety, or that I'd be writing a book or performing breakthroughs live on stage, I'd never have believed them. But this is now my reality. I'm not immune from anxiety, it still hits me from time to time, but I'm no longer limited by it. A life free from the burden of anxiety can be your reality too.

One day I stumbled upon hypnotherapy and NLP, and the rest - as they say - is history. The tools that I discovered not only helped me escape what was - in truth - a living hell but have also allowed me to gift them to so many others who have become a slave to anxiety.

NLP is the study of excellence and is fast becoming recognised as one of the best tools for personal and professional development. In a nutshell, NLP is an incredible tool that can literally re-wire your brain so that you can develop healthier habits, create deeper and more meaningful relationships (including the one with yourself), and move forward in life, no matter what obstacles you encounter along the way.

NLP is a form of psychotherapy created by Richard Bandler and John Grinder in California, USA in the 1970s, and is applied to human change, human excellence and successful communication. Much of our behaviour is driven by unconscious thought. NLP allows us to alter our behaviour and state by reorganising and disrupting our unconscious patterns. In terms of anxiety, we can use the tools to re-wire your brain and create new patterns and associations so that anxiety loses its power over you.

NLP works on the following principles:

Neuro: Your sensory experience. Each individual absorbs information through their five senses to form a sensory-based map of the outside world, consisting of images, sounds, tactile awareness, internal sensations, and tastes and smells.

Linguistic: We label what we see, hear, feel, taste and smell by comparing the immediate sensory experience with our internal maps. Our internal maps consist of recalled data, e.g. images, sounds, internal sensations, tastes and smells. We assign personal meaning by labelling it through language.

Programming: The behavioural output that occurs as a result of what has been received through the five senses (neurological processes).

I combine NLP with life coaching to motivate and offer emotional support to my clients. Life coaching can be a catalyst for facilitating change in order for you to achieve your goals and help you move forwards.

Coaching is very different from counselling. It focuses on the present and the future and identifies goals and any obstacles you are facing without dwelling on the past. Life coaching when combined with NLP and Hypnosis helps you to become the best version of you. Together we make positive changes that last a lifetime.

In this book, we are going to explore what is happening in the body during times of stress and anxiety and introduce tools to help you manage those stressful and anxious moments. We're going to examine and release some of the blocks that are stopping you from moving forward and living the life you desire, and discover the small steps you can take towards being the best version of you. I'm not offering a magic pill. I'm not saying that you will never experience anxiety again. You are, after all, human, and by the very nature of being human, you will experience anxiety, no matter how 'healed' you are. Ridding yourself of anxiety is both unnecessary and unrealistic. But what I will do is give you the tools and strategies so that you can navigate those moments and start taking control of your anxiety, instead of your anxiety controlling you.

It is possible to live with anxiety and live a normal life. It is possible to rewire your brain so that those anxious moments become less frequent and lose their grip on you. It is possible to live the life you truly desire, one that is aligned to your most authentic expression, passion and potential, even when anxiety tries to hold you back. The freedom you will get from this book is knowing that everything you need is at your fingertips and already within your reach. You already have the tools inside of you to make positive changes. This book can help you find them.

Whether you read this book from cover to cover or dip in and out as and when you need support, use this book to guide you on your journey towards freedom from anxiety.

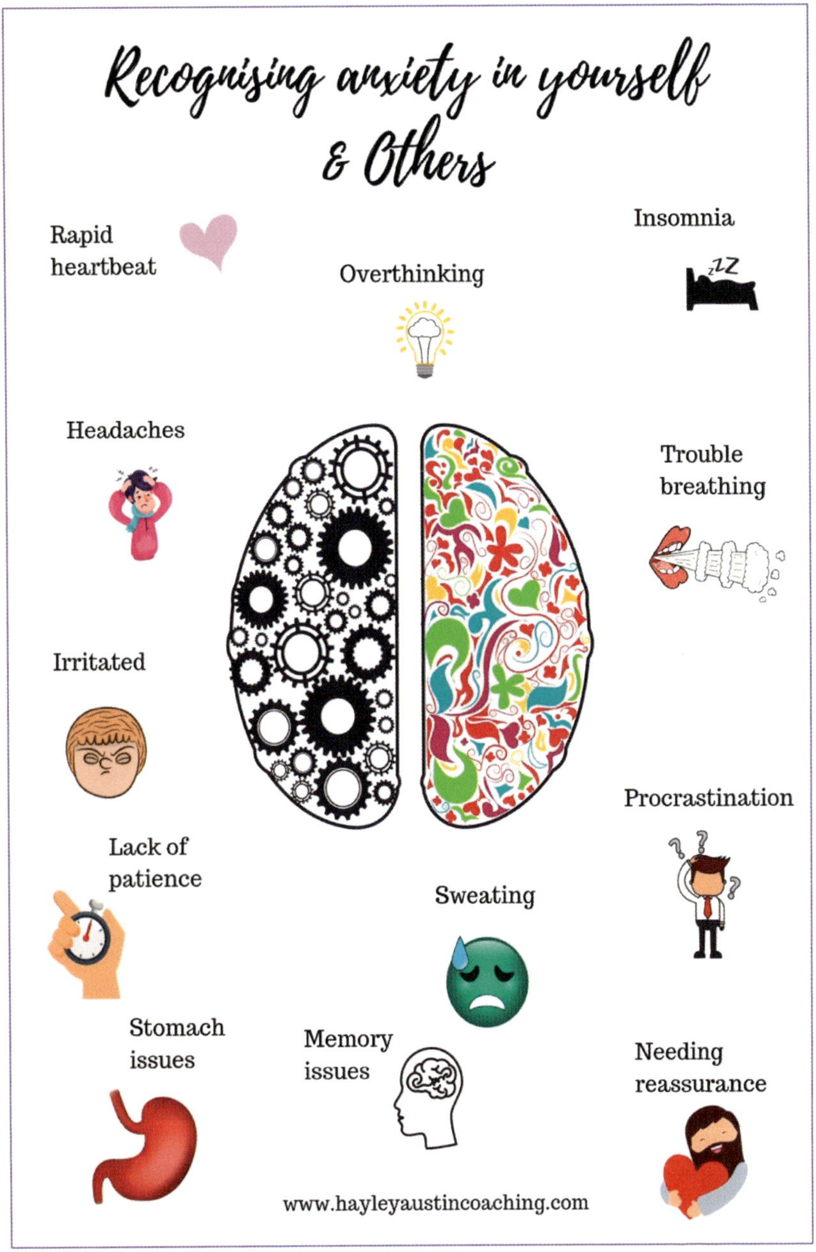
Recognising anxiety in yourself & Others
Rapid heartbeat
Overthinking
Insomnia
Headaches
Trouble breathing
Irritated
Procrastination
Lack of patience
Sweating
Stomach issues
Memory issues
Needing reassurance
www.hayleyaustincoaching.com

"My mission in life is not merely to survive, but to thrive; and to do so with some passion, some compassion, some humour, and some style."

Maya Angelou

What Are Stress & Anxiety?

My name's Hayley, and I'm a recovering anxiety warrior. I say recovering because, much like an addiction, it never truly goes away. I may not feel anxious anymore, my thoughts may no longer run away with me, but I've seen how easy it is to be seduced by those first waves. I've experienced the downward spiral as stress hits the nervous system, cortisol floods the body, and you struggle to stay afloat, let alone claw your way out. I've felt the racing heart, the sweaty palms and the inertia as I tried to hide and escape from the world.

I know how easy it is to slip back into the swamp when you don't keep on top of your mental health, something that still has so much stigma attached to it while physical wellbeing is encouraged. Luckily, I found a way out that took me on a path of self-discovery, purpose and - ultimately - freedom, and now I want to help you do the same.

I grew up not knowing my father. He was abusive towards my mother. We lived in fear of his angry outbursts, tip-toeing around him and walking on eggshells, not conducive to a happy, healthy home. When I was four-years-old, my mum arranged an escape from my dad. At the time we were living in the Isle of Man. One day my mum took my brother and me on a ferry to Heysham; that was the last we saw of my dad. We moved in with my grandma in the Lake District, back to where I was born. This was really the start of my life. My step-father came into my life when I was eleven, and while he wasn't a father-figure as such, I got used to him being around. We didn't bond on a fatherly-daughterly level, but he treated my mum well.

My mum was emotionally distant. She lacked affection, wearing armour around her heart to protect her from a harsh world. This was understandable given the way my father had treated her, albeit challenging for a growing child who needed love and validation. She didn't know how to express her love for me outwardly. She never praised me in the way I wanted. I desperately craved her attention, needing her to approve of me and make my world right, needing her to affirm my very existence. Yet she never did. Her silence was deafening. This was my perception of how I was seeing our relationship, not mum's (stay with me on this; the story unfolds and ends very well).

After finishing my high-school exams (GCSEs), I decided to go to college. My mother disapproved. She preferred for me to go to six-form to complete A-levels. However, academia wasn't my strong point. I wanted to do something more vocational and learn skills that would be better suited to me. I went against her wishes. While at college I thrived, achieving top marks, and decided to work in the hospitality industry. Mum wasn't supportive of my career choice. She didn't believe in me (or so I thought). Luckily, I still had enough belief in myself.

Aged 18 I was offered a position in a hotel which included a small salary, accommodation and fully-funded HND (Higher National Diploma) training. It was a dream come true for me. While many of my friends had set off for university and impending debts, my first thought was, 'No debt! And I won't have to ask Mum for money.' I wanted to be financially independent to prove that I didn't need anyone, to prove that I didn't need my mum, to prove to my mum that I could cope without her. I wanted her to see that I'd made the right choice and that I was successful in my own way.

I was made for hospitality. I was enthusiastic, willing to learn the ropes and my people-skills shone through. By the time I was 21 I was offered a management role in charge of the staff. Despite my success, my mum didn't show any encouragement or interest. I can see now the many ways that she tried to avoid hurt by withholding her feelings and self-expression, but at the time it felt like a major blow. I'd achieved something many 21-year-olds hadn't, yet she barely raised an eyelid. I felt deflated.

Two years later I discovered that the bar managers - my subordinates - were on a higher salary than me 'because of their age and experience'. I felt that I'd given so much yet wasn't taken seriously so decided to hand in my notice. I moved to Northampton and spent the next 11-years moving from job to job, each time acquiring new skills, taking on more responsibility and growing personally and professionally. I was living the jet-set lifestyle, spending much of my time in Morocco while managing projects and teams. I loved my life!

Then I met my first husband. We married in Italy when I was 25 but the honeymoon period soon wore off. We were too different, we didn't share the same values, and his jealousy and controlling behaviour became suffocating and started to chip away at my self-esteem. One minute life was one great high and the next it slowly began to lose its spark. Living on eggshells was the perfect breeding ground for anxiety to thrive; already those early seeds were being sowed.

We stayed together for eight years. Why did you stay with him? Why didn't you just leave? You may be asking. Because when you're living in survival mode and have lost your confidence, developing co-dependency on the very person who is bullying you, it's not that easy. Luckily, I started to see the light. I slowly regained my confidence and realised that I deserved better. I also met a man who showed me that I was worthy of love and affection, that I no longer needed to buy into the story of unworthiness that my husband had fed me and that I could create a new one. And so, I did. Looking back, I can now see that mine and my ex-husband's values weren't aligned. We didn't want the same things, and we were no longer in love.

I left my ex for my current husband who I met at work, my knight in shining armour. As much as it's no one else's responsibility to rescue us, sometimes it takes another person's belief in you to help you climb out of a hole.

Our relationship was frowned upon, what with him being on the board of directors, but I loved my job regardless. As operations manager, I travelled all over Asia. I felt that, with this burgeoning relationship, my toxic marriage behind me and my career at an all-time high, I was living the dream. I was feeling confident again. I was starting to feel better about myself and love the person reflected back at me in the mirror. Things were on the up. Yet the one person I still couldn't impress was my mum. She remained passive, stoic and indifferent. This was the moment that I realised that I would never make my mum proud (at least, that's what I believed in my mind). All those years of desperately trying to get positive attention or some kind of reaction from her, waiting to hear 'I'm proud of you Hayley,' words that never came. I'd spent the best years of my life working to better myself, advancing in my career and ticking all the success boxes to get some kind of feedback and approval from my mum. This was the moment I decided to live my life for me and released the need to please others.

I fell pregnant quickly which was a shock - even though it was planned - gave birth to my son Jacob, and then got married in Vegas when Jacob was just 4-months old. Life as a new mum was lonely. I'd lost all of my friends when I left my ex-husband. They were his circle of friends and my own friends I'd already left behind when he became more controlling in our relationship. My work colleagues ostracised me after I sued the company for discrimination. I had no one, not even my mum who rarely visited. I couldn't enjoy my son. I didn't want to go to any baby groups. I felt paranoid that people were judging me because here I was with a newborn and a much older man. It didn't feel safe to go out. I feared being confronted by old friends who would not take kindly to my new marriage and baby, so I either stayed in or went to a different part of town. The first onset of anxiety came creeping in, and before long it was crippling.

Every time I plucked up the courage to go out, I'd backtrack before I'd even had a chance to step outside. My stomach would tighten, and it would spread to my chest. My heart would start racing, my hands would become sweaty, and nausea would kick in. I'd second-guess myself and make excuses, using my baby as the perfect reason not to do anything. Jacob will need feeding so I might as well stay in, I'd convince myself. When I did go out, I'd drive and become an anxious mess. Sometimes my hands would shake so much that I had to pull over. The more I retreated from the world, the more isolated I felt and the more anxious I became. This continued for nine months.

I didn't speak to my GP or my husband about how I felt. It was like a dirty little secret that only I knew. I felt ashamed. My mind wouldn't switch off, and my thoughts became more and more irrational, yet still, I couldn't tell anyone. I was so used to being in control and having it all together that now I felt like a fraud. I didn't want to be seen as weak, a failure or an unfit mum. I thought that everyone would judge me, including my husband. I honestly didn't think anyone would be able to help. In truth, I didn't believe that other people could possibly feel the way that I did. I thought it was just me.

Turning my anxiety around took a massive leap of faith which I will discuss later on in this book. Suffice to say, I wasn't alone in my struggle. Stress and anxiety are far more common than we think. We all suffer from anxiety at some point in our lives. And the best bit? You don't have to suffer alone as I did. The more we break the stigma and talk about our personal struggles with mental health, the more we realise just how common it is. Thankfully advances in neuroscience mean that we have a greater understanding of what's happening inside our brains and body when we're experiencing anxiety. We have access to more tools and healing modalities such as NLP and hypnotherapy to help us work through our stress and alleviate the symptoms as they arise. While medication is often demonised, it's readily available and helps take the edge off and can be the catalyst some people need to seek help. The first step is to acknowledge your struggle, own it without attaching any shame or judgment to it, and then take the necessary action to help you work through it. I want to emphasise here that asking for help is not a weakness. In fact, it's the most courageous thing to do.

What is Stress?

Before I continue, I want to reassure you that stress is a perfectly normal and healthy response. We are wired for stress, an in-built system that has served to protect us since our primitive days when the fight-or-flight response kept us safe from real threat. Today, the threat may not be real - much of it is perceived - but the response is the same; our amygdala (or threat detector) doesn't discriminate. However, when left unmanaged, stress can become unhealthy and manifest as unwanted behaviours, dis-ease, IBS, weight issues, apathy, loss of libido and much more. See figure 1.0 on page 19 to see the impact of stress on the body.

We have become so accepting of stress that weeks, months and sometimes years can pass before we feel inclined to do something about it. Often we ignore it until it's too late and we find ourselves unable to cope and in need of medical intervention. Society sells 'busy-ness' as a badge of honour. We push and strive, overschedule ourselves and our kids, burn the candle at both ends and attach our level of 'doing' to our measure of worth. Do nothing or have no plans and you're judged as lazy or dull. Little wonder that people struggle to seek help for stress-related symptoms when culture perpetuates it.

During a stress response, your brain produces adrenaline. You know that sudden rush of energy? That's the adrenaline kicking in to prepare you to fight, flee or freeze. How we respond to stress is different for everyone. Some people panic and want to run away while others seem to find an inner grit and altruistic quality to risk their lives and save others (firefighters are the perfect example of this). Whatever your natural response, do not attach any shame or judgment around this. We all at some point fantasise about being the hero of the hour, but the reality is that we're not all built that way. When adrenaline surges, we are reactive, not responsive, and our physiology takes over. We go into autopilot, and our conscious mind shuts down, all with the very best of intentions to keep us safe. How incredible is the human body!

Adrenaline is swiftly followed by the secretion of cortisol to relax and calm the body. Healthy adrenal glands will secrete cortisol according to circadian rhythm - our natural eat and sleep cycle - encoded in us to follow the 24-hour rhythm of the sun. Rising cortisol levels help us wake up in the morning while levels drop as we approach bedtime. Ever noticed that you wake earlier in the summer while starting to feel tired earlier in the winter? That's your circadian rhythm at play. We all have our own rhythm, yet modern life rarely honours our natural cycles. We often eat when we're not hungry because work or family life dictates mealtimes. Our waking hour is typically defined by an alarm and schedule, instead of allowing the process to occur naturally. Demands and expectations often leave us overworked, wired, with very little time for rest and play. We find ourselves in a constant state of stress with adrenaline flooding our body, our adrenals producing excessive amounts of cortisol which - ultimately - become fatigued.

There are three stages of stress - alarm, resistance and exhaustion - that are explained in further detail below. From these descriptions, we can quickly see how stress can escalate when we don't address it in the earlier stages.

Stage 1 (alarm) – the stress response is designed to be temporary. Adrenaline and cortisol elevate and then stop when the stressor has passed. When we experience stress for extended periods than is considered 'normal' or temporary, we start to feel wired. We experience feelings of overwhelm, fear and panic. We experience paranoia and anxiety. We feel as though we're losing control so try to control everything and everyone around us, only to feel more out of control than before. Our self-esteem and confidence start to nose-dive, we become fidgety, irritable and feel on edge. We become more explosive in our reactions, so our relationships begin to suffer. Migraines and GI problems including IBS flare up. These symptoms all serve as a warning sign, however, often we don't acknowledge or recognise the stress that underpins them.

Stage 2 (resistance) – cortisol remains elevated while DHEA production (a naturally occurring steroid in humans, produced in the adrenal glands) declines to below normal. We may start to experience long-term, prolonged stress, sudden weight gain or loss, insomnia, increased emotional eating or drinking and a feeling of living in survival mode. We may experience high blood pressure, addictions, OCD, and increased libido. We may also experience feeling hyperactive yet exhausted at the same time. Most people are at this stage at the time of seeking help.

Stage 3 (exhaustion) – output of cortisol and DHEA is below normal. By this point, we're physically, mentally and emotionally exhausted. Adrenal fatigue (burnout) is common at this stage. We may experience depression, low blood pressure, low tolerance to cold and low libido. We may struggle to get out of bed; everything feels such an effort. We can develop chronic fatigue syndrome, hypothyroidism, asthma and eczema. This stage of stress is profoundly debilitating, and intervention is required, typically in the form of medication. Many people at this stage are signed off from work for several months.

Figure 1.0 – The Effects of Stress on Your Body

The Importance of Sleep

If you are dealing with stress, feeling anxious and under pressure, chances are your sleep will be poor. Overthinking stops the brain from shutting down making it difficult to enter the sleep cycle and stay in it!

Sleep plays a vital role in your physical health. For example, sleep aids the healing and repair of your heart and blood vessels. Ongoing sleep deficiency is linked to an increased risk of heart disease, kidney disease, high blood pressure, diabetes, and stroke.

Sleep is as important to our health as eating, drinking and breathing. Poor sleep is linked to physical problems such as a weakened immune system and mental health problems such as anxiety and depression.

Studies show people who are sleep deprived report increases in negative moods (anger, frustration, irritability, sadness) and decreases in positive moods. Your mood can affect how well you sleep, while your quality of sleep can affect your mood; it's a vicious cycle.

The body moves through five different stages of REM (rapid eye movement) and NREM (non-rapid eye movement) sleep. The body will go through this five-stage cycle four to six times throughout the night, spending an average of 90 minutes in each stage. It is essential to allow enough time to cycle through all sleep stages as each one serves a unique restorative function. Without a full night of good-quality sleep, these functions are impaired, impacting your general mood and wellbeing the following day.

Stage 1: Stage one of sleep - the transitional phase - occurs when you float in and out of consciousness. This is when your mind begins to drift off, eventually leading into a light sleep. After winding down in stage one, you will then enter stage 2 of the sleep cycle.

Stage 2: Stage two is also a non-REM phase and is one of the lighter stages of sleep. During stage two, eye movement stops and brain waves slow with the occasional burst of waves called sleep spindles.

Stages 3 & 4: Stages three and four are the deep stages of sleep. They are the hardest to wake up from. If you wake up disoriented and groggy, it's likely you've woken up during one of these stages. Stages three and four are the periods of slow wave sleep - when the brain waves slow to what is known as delta waves, with the occasional faster wave. As the body moves from stage three to four, the number of delta waves increase, and the faster waves decrease. During slow wave sleep, the body becomes immobile, and there is no eye movement. Nightmares, bedwetting and sleepwalking occur during slow wave sleep as the muscles can still function.

Stages three and four of sleep are extremely important for rejuvenating the body. During slow wave sleep, hormones are released that aid in both growth and appetite control. When sleep is disrupted and these stages limited, subsequent overeating is common.

Stage 5: Stage five is the only stage of rapid eye movement (REM) and serves to revitalise the brain, supporting sharp and alert daytime functioning. During this phase, the brain is bursting with activity. During non-REM sleep, the mind rests while the body heals, while in REM sleep the mind energises itself while the body is immobile. Most dreaming takes place in stage five as a result of heightened brain waves, almost similar to being awake. We typically wake up at the end of this stage.

We have five brain wave states: delta, theta, alpha, beta and gamma. Each brain wave has a distinct electrical pattern and purpose and helps us behave, think, move and process. Deep meditation produces theta waves. The period when we drift in and out of sleep, and our thoughts feel dreamlike and difficult to remember, is when we're in a theta-dominant state of consciousness. Delta waves begin to emerge during this period to transition us from light to very deep sleep. This is one of the reasons why meditation is so effective, especially when used as a sleep aid.

Exercise: Are you getting enough sleep?

Ask yourself these questions and be honest.

- How much sleep do you get every day?
- How much caffeine do you have a day? Include coffee, fizzy drinks etc
- How much alcohol do you drink per week?
- Do you smoke and, if yes, how much?
- How often do you exercise?
- What is your diet like?

Your answers to these questions can give a great indication into the quality of your sleep, especially when used alongside any symptoms of sleep deprivation you may have. Stimulants such as tobacco, alcohol and sugar do not help with stress or anxiety while lack of exercise inhibits the release of feel-good hormones, endorphins, dopamine and serotonin. Diet plays a huge role in physical and mental health. When we don't get enough sleep, we tend to reach for unhealthier food options, foods that in turn can negatively impact our sleep.

Here are some useful tips to improve the quality of your sleep:

- **Create a sleep schedule** using the same bedtime and wake up time, and stick to it, however tempting it is to have a lie in at the weekend! Over time this will help you to regulate your body clock as your body will start to expect to sleep and wake at specific times.

- **Create a bedtime ritual** to help you relax and prepare you for sleep. This could mean having a hot bath with lavender oils, switching off screens an hour before bed, having a cup of chamomile tea and reading a book. Experiment to see what activities work to get you into a relaxed and sleepy state.

- **Avoid afternoon naps** if you have trouble sleeping. If you're a napper and find that you can't fall asleep at bedtime, eliminating a power nap may help.

- **Exercise daily**, at any time of day, but not at the expense of your sleep.

- **Adjust your sleep environment** to create the conditions you need for sleep. Your bedroom should be cool and free from any noise that can disturb your sleep. Consider using blackout curtains, eye shades, ear plugs, fans and other devices to make your room more comfortable.

- **Check your bedding.** Make sure your mattress and pillows are comfortable and supportive. If you find you frequently wake with a sore back, it could be time to invest in a new mattress!

- **Be mindful of what you eat and drink.** Alcohol, cigarettes and caffeine can disrupt sleep; avoid them! Eating big or spicy meals too close to bedtime can cause digestive discomfort. If you can, avoid eating large meals for two to three hours before bedtime. A small snack such as a banana can be consumed 45 minutes before bed if you find you're still hungry.

- **Keep computers and televisions out of the sleeping environment.** If you associate a particular activity with anxiety about sleeping, remove it from your bedtime routine.

My intention for this book is to give you the tools to help alleviate your symptoms of stress during stage 1. I want you to see the importance of self-care in a world that has taught you to put your own needs last. I want you to recognise your value and worth and start addressing the deeper issues that are contributing to your stress. I want you to start paying attention to the warning signs so that you never have to experience stage three (or even stage 2). And, most importantly, I want you to know that you're not alone on this journey.

Before we dive deeper, let's take a look at some quick-fixes to help in those more immediate stressful moments.

Short-term Strategies for Stress and Anxiety

Breathe. Never underestimate the power of your breath. It is available to you at all times and is an incredibly powerful way of calming your nervous system. Remember, during the stress response, your body is flooded with cortisol. Breathing becomes shallow and less oxygen reaches your brain. Focus on your breathing. Take long, deep and slow breaths. Not only are you altering your physiology but by focusing on your breathing, you're distracting yourself from the conscious (and unconscious) thoughts that are contributing to your stress.

Breathing Exercise 1: Focus your attention on your breath. Breathe in slowly for 6 seconds, hold for 4 seconds, then exhale for 5 seconds. Repeat this three times.

Breathing Exercise 2: Anxiety thrusts us into a future state so the quickest way to ease it is to get back into the present moment. Do this by actively engaging your five senses. Look around you and note five things that you see, four things that you hear, three things you can feel/touch, two things you can smell, and one thing you can taste. By focusing on your senses, you immediately become more present and distracted from your thoughts. The beauty of this process is that it can be followed anywhere, at any time.

Identify your stage of stress. If you're at stage 3, seek medical help. If you're at stages 1 and 2 and know that fear, mental blocks or trauma underlies your stress, try the following exercise(s):

NLP Techniques for dissolving fear, mental blocks and hesitation

NLP anchors are among the most useful NLP techniques. When you understand anchoring and have practised it, you can change your state whenever you need to. Feel free to connect with me and I will do a video demonstration with you.

Exercise: Stacking the anchors

Firstly, think of a time when you had a block on something you wanted to do.

Perhaps you couldn't bring yourself to apply for the promotion you really felt you deserved, or you couldn't motivate yourself to go to the gym and get into shape. Perhaps you are to provide a talk and cannot face going onto the stage.

Picture it very clearly in your mind. See what you can see. Make the picture bright, 3D and full of colour.

Feel the feelings you associated with it at the time. Go deep inside your unconscious mind and connect with the feeling. The feeling may be in your tummy like butterflies. Listen to any sounds or feelings associated with it. As soon as it is really clear, anchor it on some part of your body. To do this, tap on a particular place on your wrist as these feelings increase. Or make the ok sign using your left hand by squeezing your middle finger and thumb together.

Think of any other times you had a block and perform the same routine of seeing it, feeling it and hearing it, and stack the anchors in the same position - on the left hand again, squeezing the middle finger and thumb together.

Then think of the desire and frustration you felt at not doing these things and stack those anchors.

Now, think of a time when you actually did go for something you wanted.

You may have to dig deep, and it may not seem significant to you now, but there was a time in your life when you did that.

Make a large picture in your mind, see what you saw, hear what you heard, and feel what you felt.

Make the picture a movie and see yourself going for whatever it was. Make the colours sharp, 3D, and bright. There may be some familiar smells around you, e.g. your favourite perfume or aftershave. Notice the way you are moving with confidence and what you were wearing. Really get inside the feeling you are experiencing right now.

Let the feeling of satisfaction overwhelm you, and as it does so anchor it on a different part of your body. Use your right hand and squeeze together your middle finger and thumb as the feelings intensify.

The next stage is to fire the first anchor and, as you do so, think of the times when you blocked yourself from going for your goals. To fire the anchor, create an ok sign with your finger and thumb and squeeze together really tight as the feelings develop, then fire by releasing your finger and thumb.

As the feeling builds up inside you, fire the second anchor and hold both anchors together for a moment before releasing the first anchor. As you release the first anchor, notice the feelings of doubt disappear.

Now fire the first anchor and hold it until it triggers desire and frustration and then fire those anchors and as the feelings build, hold and fire the second anchor.

Repeat that process until you feel a real desire to take action.

Exercise: Removing mental blocks.

Designed by Stephen J Ruden and Ronald A Ruden.

Please read the instructions through from beginning to end to make sure you understand them fully before starting the exercise. Remember practice makes perfect. You will need to practice these exercises daily until you have mastered the anchoring process. A very relaxing technique that you will find valuable.

Firstly, think about the block you have and consider how badly you feel about it.

Rate that on a scale of 1 to 10 (10 being the worst) so that you can measure your improvement.

Now clear your mind and think of something pleasant.

Next use both hands and tap on both your collar bones.

While you continue tapping on both collar bones, keep your head still, look straight ahead and close and open your eyes.

While you continue tapping and holding your head still, look down to the left and then down to the right.

Keep tapping. Keep your head still. Move your eyes in a full circle clockwise and then anti-clockwise.

Next, cross your arms, place each hand on the top of your shoulders and close your eyes.

Stroke your hands down the sides of your arms from your shoulders to your elbows and back again and again.

As you stroke the sides of your arms, imagine you are walking down a flight of stairs and count out loud from 1 to 20 with each step you take. When you reach 20, hum or sing the first two or three lines of Happy Birthday.

Let your arms go back down to your sides, relax, open your eyes and look up in front of and above you. Then move your eyes slowly from left to right and back three times.

Close your eyes, breathe in deeply, exhale and stroke your arms again in the same fashion a further five times.

Open your eyes. Think about your block and rate your block on the scale of 1 to 10 and see how much it has reduced. If it is not reduced as far as you would like it to be, repeat the exercise from beginning to end.

It is worth adding that you can perform this exercise in almost any stressful situation you can imagine, for example, going to the dentist, or before you are about to speak in public.

It is well worth practising it repeatedly until it becomes second nature. It may also become your best friend.

Richard Bandler, co-originator of NLP, first devised this technique for fast phobia cure. It also works extremely well for general fear and trauma.

Please note that I normally use this technique alongside hypnosis for the greatest effect. It can be used consciously (outside of hypnosis) but I'd recommend going through the deep breathing exercise first. Below is a simplified way to help you with fears and phobias. For trauma, skip to option two which is slightly different. You may want to ask someone to read it for you so that you can work through the exercise.

First of all, I want you to take a deep breath in through your nose and hold for the count of three. I then want you to exhale through your mouth and count to five. Repeat this three times, or until you can feel your body and mind start to relax. This technique will restore your oxygen levels, slow your heart rate and help you feel calm. You must be in a relaxed state to benefit from the exercise.

Exercise: Fast Phobia Cure

Think of a time you faced fear. I want you to create a story with a beginning, middle and an end. Make sure your story has a happy ending with your safe place, the place that you felt safe and secure once your feelings of fear passed.

Get inside the memory - step into it as if it is happening right here and now - and notice what you can see, smell, feel and hear. Connect with all of your senses. Score the fear between 0 - 10 (10 being highest).

In your mind I want you to visualise your favourite cinema. Perhaps it's a cinema you went to when you were younger. You know the ones - sticky carpets, the smell of popcorn and people talking. Now walk into the cinema and find a seat. I want you to take a seat and look at the screen.

Before the movie of your fear starts, I want you to float out of your body and up into the projector booth. Look out into the auditorium and see yourself sat in the chair about to watch your 'fear' movie. It is important to visualise this correctly so that you can disassociate yourself away from the fear.

a) Run a black and white movie of the event on the movie screen.

b) Watch the whole event starting before the beginning of the fear response, through to the moment after the event when you felt better. Make it a black and white movie with sound, running at normal speed.

c) Observe your younger self going through the experience. Watch the movie as a detached observer, even as a stranger. As needed, emphasise that you are safe, here and now, safe in the booth, feeling the glass with your hands, while also noticing the other self in the theatre seat watching. It's just a movie.

d) Run the movie to the end of the situation and stop the film on the last frame, like a snapshot.

Well done, stay with me.

Leave the booth and float quickly into your former self in the still picture on the screen. When fully there, run the movie backwards all the way to the beginning, in colour, in about two seconds. Make a sound to indicate this: 'Just run it back real fast…shooouuup!'.

When you have done it, test your responses. Ask a question that would have elicited the fear response. If there is still is a reaction, check the way you ran the process. Take yourself back through it, making sure you do it correctly. Repeat as necessary. Practice makes perfect!

Tip… As you run the movie backwards in colour, try singing circus music to yourself as you rewind faster and faster - this confuses the memory.

Encourage yourself to take your time to carefully understand and accept better choices of response in future possible similar situations, as appropriate. Re-score your phobia.

Technically, utilising the phobia cure for trauma is simply a matter of combining it with regression (using timeline or any other regression theatrics). Take yourself back to the incident - but floating safely above it - and run phobia theatre while floating in the air over the incident at this safe distance, running a movie of the incident.

Like all techniques, they need to be practised over and over again. Mastering these enables you to change your state quickly and effectively.

I am not a medical doctor and I do not specialise in mental illness. While NLP techniques can powerfully transform anxiety, depression, PTSD and trauma, this won't be true for everyone. Therapy and medical assistance are sometimes the most appropriate interventions, especially when dealing with deep trauma.

A Look Inside the Brain

Anxiety is a complex emotional response which has two pathways in the brain: the cerebral cortex (responsible for our perceptions and thoughts) and the amygdala (the 'fight-or-flight' centre). The cortex is the uppermost part of the brain, typically known as the 'thinking' brain. This is where reasoning and logic are formed. The cortex can cause, increase or decrease anxiety depending on our thinking at any moment. Consciously changing our thoughts can alter cognitive processes and start to lay down new pathways (which is why journaling can be so powerful. See more on this in chapter 4).

The amygdala is the more primitive part of the brain and influences our ability to love and bond, aggression and sexual behaviour, anger and fear. The amygdala attaches emotional significance to people, objects and situations and creates an emotional response and subsequent behaviours.

In times of stress, the amygdala is on high alert to detect threat and danger. It sends a message to the sympathetic nervous system to protect you from attack. The nervous system responds by increasing heart rate and pumping cortisol around your body. Blood is diverted to the brain, heart, lungs and muscles to prepare you for fight, flee or even freeze during times of danger. Once the threat has passed, the system returns to normal.

The cortex can trigger the amygdala. When we think about our worries and fears, our amygdala detects our thoughts and the stress response kicks in. Much like a smoke alarm can't distinguish between a real fire and burnt toast, the amygdala cannot distinguish between what is real and what is not; it detects fear and reacts, as nature intended. In times of anxiety, there is an absence of real threat. Our thought processes create a feeling of fear - e.g. worrying about being late for work or speaking in public - even though there is no real threat at that moment. Whether there is a real threat, e.g. someone is chasing you, or a perceived threat, e.g. the thought of someone chasing you (when they're not), the response is the same.

When we have a negative emotional experience, our cortex applies logic and meaning and therefore integrates and processes our experience fully. When we're not able to fully process a negative emotion, e.g. the fear surrounding physical violence, we suppress that emotion, and it continues to be triggered during times of stress. Trauma underlies a lot of anxiety at a very unconscious level. When your fears appear irrational, there's a high chance that unresolved trauma and negative emotions are driving those anxieties.

20 Ways to Improve Your Wellbeing

Our physical health has a significant impact on our mental and emotional health. How we treat ourselves and fuel our body can alter our physiology and therefore increase or decrease our stress levels. Small acts of kindness to ourselves are fundamental to our overall wellbeing, however, many of us make self-care the last on our list of priorities. We have been conditioned to believe that focusing on our own needs is selfish, indulgent and self-absorbed, when the opposite is true. Self-care is an act of self-love: when we take care of ourselves, everyone benefits! The small steps you take towards your own self-care can radically shift the feelings of low self-esteem and self-worth that many of us carry (more of this in chapter 6 – *Connection with Self (and the world)*) and alter the relationship you have with yourself and those around you. Luckily, there are some very simple changes that can have a profound impact, as you will discover in the list below. Take baby steps, incorporate the suggestions that most resonate, and repeat daily until they become a habit.

1. Eat Berries for Breakfast

Berries are an incredible food, rich in nutrients for our brain, our digestion, and they're disease-preventative. They're also a fresh source of produce and keep us fuller than processed cereals with dried fruits. Add 1/2 cup of your choice frozen or fresh berries to either a smoothie, oatmeal, or just have some with some unsweetened coconut yoghurt and a little chia or flax seeds. Berries are also a great source of vitamin C to kickstart your immune system.

2. Eat One Green Food Every Day

Eating one green vegetable per day or one leafy green is a great way to get yourself healthier in the kitchen without much thought. It can be a cup of broccoli at dinner or adding spinach to your smoothie. Anything counts, just make sure it's green, natural, and from the earth. These foods provide us with more nutrition than any food out there. They alkalise our bodies, promote mental wellness, and protect us from disease.

3. Drink a Glass of Water When You Wake Up

A new health practice that many observe, drinking water is essential to hydrating your body first thing in the day after a night-long fast. It helps wake you up and is an excellent way to flush out your body first thing to keep you regular, a crucial part of staying healthy. Dehydration has a significant impact on moods. If you're feeling lethargic or grumpy, it could be that you need to up your water intake. Your body contains (and needs) more water than most of us realise. Be sure you're giving it enough, starting first thing — even before the coffee!

4. Enjoy Tea and Coffee

Coffee and tea are two of the most amazing sources of antioxidants in our diet, so long as they're sustainably (preferably) organically sourced, so they're produced without pesticides. These two beverages boost mental health, liver health, and promote a healthy heart. The key is to leave out the sugar and milk, which takes away most all their benefits. Coffee has been studied recently for its impact on longevity and cancer prevention, while tea has been a long-standing healing remedy for years.

5. Cook Your Own Meals

Cooking at home can not only be incredibly therapeutic and a great mindfulness tool, but you have more control over the quality of food that you eat. Start to cook more at home, even if it means preparing simple meals such as soup, throwing a recipe in the slow cooker, whipping up a protein with vegetables, or even some smoothies with oatmeal for a fun breakfast option. If you're able, try batch cooking at the weekend and freezing your meals to save time during the week. The key here is to start slowly and find a realistic way to work around your other commitments; you don't need to cook everything from scratch.

6. Use Herbs Instead of Salt

Salt is a great flavour enhancer, but in excess, it burdens the liver. Instead of shaking salt on all your food, try using herbs as an alternative way to flavour them. For breakfast, use cinnamon, cardamom and ginger for a sweet and spicy flavour. For lunch, use Italian seasonings, sage, black pepper, and/or cayenne and turmeric. For dinner, try some garam masala,

pepper, oregano, basil, and thyme. If you're not ready to ditch the salt just yet, ensure you switch to a high-quality sea or rock salt.

7. Ditch the Sugar

Sugary foods are not part of a healthy diet, mostly because they're processed, void of nutrients, and can be addictive; the reward centres of our brain love sugar, as do our taste buds. Instead of choosing something with sugar, have an apple, some berries, a banana, an orange, or just enjoy sweet veggies like carrots instead. Your body will learn to love the taste of fresh vegetables and fruits when you give it a chance. Sugar ages your skin, messes with your digestion, makes you moody, tired, and doesn't satisfy your appetite. Psychologically, sugar cravings are often associated with a lack of 'sweetness' in our life. If this resonates, explore ways that you can bring more fun, play and joy into your life.

8. Aim for 30-minutes of Fitness a Day

This might sound difficult, but it is easier than we all think. Getting up just 30 minutes earlier in the morning will give you plenty of time to get in a walk (or jog). If you like to run, even better, but walking is excellent too. Moving first thing in the day boosts your serotonin levels, provides energy to the body, and also helps you focus better throughout the day. It is also an easy way to improve your metabolism to help manage your weight.

9. Don't Stay Seated Too

Sitting is not as evil as it's being made out to be now, but it is vital that we don't 'over sit' our welcome. We need to stand more throughout the day, even if that's while chatting with friends, talking on the phone, or just getting up in between nightly relaxing activities before bed. If you like to watch television, be sure not to sit there for hours on end while doing so. If you work at a computer all day, get up and move around or try to stand and work however possible.

10. Spend Time Outside

Take a stroll around your neighbourhood or walk through a local park each day if you live near one. If you have a dog, take them for a five-minute walk down the street. If you have the option to exercise outside, give it a go; it's rejuvenating compared to indoor treadmills! Being active outside, even just for a few minutes, is a great way to enlighten your spirits without trying. It puts you in touch with nature, which studies show can actually benefit our brains, prevent depression, and exposes us to the most natural source of vitamin D available to us: the sun.

11. Try Yoga

While yoga isn't for everyone, its many benefits are so profound that we should all at least give it a shot. Don't let yoga intimidate you if it seems out of reach or strange. It's actually just a fluid way of moving your body, stretching everything out, and being kinder to your body through movement. While a gruelling workout at the gym is great for pumping muscles, yoga is a nice change of pace that reduces cortisol in the body. This lowers stress around the clock and reduces insulin spikes caused by elevated cortisol levels.

12. Do Something You Love Everyday

This can be something as small as cooking your favourite breakfast, writing in a journal a few minutes a day, participating in a local event or a favourite hobby, or anything else that you genuinely love. Doing something small for yourself every day is a great way to enhance serotonin levels in the body and raise those feel-good hormones on a regular basis.

13. Eat Good Fats

Healthy fats are like fuel for a good mood. They're one of the most important things to include in your diet to promote a good mood (and a balanced metabolism). Healthy fats also promote good heart health, reduce cholesterol, and contain none of the harmful side effects associated with animal-based saturated fats. Go for raw coconut, avocados, almonds, walnuts, acai fruit, flax seeds, cashews, hemp seeds, chia seeds, pumpkin seeds, sesame seeds or tahini, pecans, and olives. Many of these are also packed with protein, B vitamins, and magnesium to enhance brain health.

14. Ditch the Negative Self-Talk

Consistently telling yourself reasons why you can't do something, don't deserve something, or will never achieve something will not get you to where you want to be. Ditch the negative self-talk and start creating new messages instead. When you change your mindset, you have the power to change your life. This is one of the most overlooked - yet powerful -ways to improve mood and mental health daily.

15. Get Social

Social wellness is something most of us don't pay enough attention to, but we should for long-term health. Even if you enjoy alone time, keep in mind that we are all social creatures by nature. Humans need connection (as you will discover in chapter 2). Social interaction isn't a privilege, it's a necessity. Human contact can relieve stress, enhance our mood, and even promote longevity. Spending time with friends, family, or chatting with someone at the gym, park, or the office is a crucial way to stroke your social needs daily.

16. Learn to Love Sleep

Why has sleep become something we have to work into our schedules? Sleep is a gift, something that's just as important as the food on our plate and our exercise habits. It's the time of the day that our body resets itself, detoxifies, and enables us to conquer the next day ahead. Depression, weight gain, stress, and even food cravings can all occur when we don't get enough rest. Some of us need more or less sleep than others. Don't fixate on how much sleep you think you need — get enough until you wake up at the same time each day without the need for an alarm clock.

17. Become a Minimalist

In a world of chaos and clutter, never underestimate the power simplification! Having beautiful things is great, and such a treat to give ourselves whenever we can, however, we should always remember the joy that being a minimalist can bring to our lives.

Sometimes less is more, and the little things often give us the most joy. Cut down on the number of products you use or learn to prepare more simple meals. Try scaling down your wardrobe and donating what you no longer wear. Ditch the pricey beauty products and use more natural options instead. Clean out your kitchen and stick to whole foods with simple preparation tips. Look at your spending habits and the intention behind them: is what you're buying a genuine want or need, or are you using it to fill a void or meet a deeper need? Living a simpler life can make you healthier and happier without the need for so much 'stuff'.

18. Try a New Activity Each Month

Our schedules can turn us into creatures of habit. A life lacking interest or variety can leave us feeling bored, unhappy, and possibly lose our passion for things we care about such as being active, our jobs, and even our healthy eating habits. Try a new activity when you can, possibly once a month. This can be something as simple as cooking an original recipe, trying a new exercise, working in a different atmosphere, attending a different exercise class, or even just shopping at a local farmer's market instead of a retail store.

19. Practice Positivity

No matter what we have going on in our lives, one of the most important things we can all do is bring energy, not steal it. This means maintaining a positive outlook and energy, even if our lives are not how we think they should be. This is important for our health, along with the health of others around us. People who have a positive spirit can make a significant impact on people around them. If everyone practised positivity, the world would be a happier place. This isn't to say that you can't experience low moods or negative emotions: honour your feelings but make a conscious choice not to dwell there. The next place you go to, even if it's a meeting at work you're dreading, bring energy and positivity into the room instead of stealing it away with a negative outlook. Smile more at strangers; positivity radiates and has a ripple effect. A simple smile can lift someone else's mood and shift the trajectory of their day!

20. Have a Morning Routine

If you work out in the morning, this is an opportunity to get some quiet time to yourself. If you don't already have a morning routine, incorporate this into your day so that you get some quiet alone time. This can help reduce the stress hormone cortisol in the body, which peaks first thing in the morning. It also gives you time to ground yourself and prepare yourself mentally before the busyness of the day ahead. You might like to write out your thoughts, to-do's, prayers, concerns, or whatever else comes to mind upon waking – do what works for you. Having just 10 minutes to yourself each morning, perhaps over coffee, is a simple way to incorporate self-care into your day.

"The most difficult thing is the decision to act; the rest is merely tenacity. The fears are paper tigers. You can do anything you decide to do."

Amelia Earhart

Who Are You?

Who am I and why am I here? is the all elusive existential question many of us ask ourselves at some point in our lives. Indeed, it often takes years of soul-searching and examining our experiences and beliefs before we start to discover who we really are beneath the facade we've created. Society has a way of telling us to be ourselves yet applies conditions as to who we need to be to be accepted. We learn that we need to think, feel and act the same to fit in and belong, denying our quirks, disregarding our values and disconnecting from the voice inside that knows we belong. Many of us are on a quest to rediscover ourselves by seeking the answers on the outside. In this chapter, we are going to take a journey within ourselves to find who we've been looking for.

I spent a lot of my time thinking I knew who I was yet discovered I was striving to be who I thought my mum wanted me to be. Don't get me wrong, I enjoyed my life and career. I had some incredible experiences and met my current husband through work. However, I strived for what I thought was my mum's version of success, so desperate was I for her approval.

When I became a mum, I started to feel lost. I didn't know who I was anymore or who I was supposed to be in this new role. One minute I was a high-flying, self-assured career woman and the next my whole life and responsibilities changed. The things that were important before no longer mattered. My value system was turned upside-down. Sometimes I'd glance in the mirror, and it felt like a stranger was staring back at me. Who am I without the identity I'd worked so hard to create? Why did my life no longer fit? It didn't help that anxiety really took hold around this time, fuelling the confusion.

I no longer wanted to be in the corporate rat-race. When once it thrilled me, it now repelled me. I didn't want to travel. I didn't want to be away from my son. But there was a part of that wanted to do something. I had a deep knowing that there was something else waiting for me. Clouded in anxiety, the thought of stepping out of my comfort zone scared me. I needed certainty, to feel safe. As it stood, I could barely leave the house most days.

My husband worked away a lot, so it was just Jacob and me at home. I felt lonely and missed adult company. I missed the connection. Eventually, we relocated to Huddersfield. The move transformed my life.

While I didn't know anybody, Huddersfield felt safe. I was no longer at risk of bumping into anyone from my past, so little by little I restored my courage and stepped out of the house, soaking in my new surroundings. I still felt lonely, but it felt different. It had lost its edge. If anything, I felt hopeful. I could look more positively towards the future knowing that I'd made a fresh start. The anxiety started to ease its grip as I began to relax into my new life.

But still, I craved connection. As much as I cherished my son, I desired adult friendship. And more than that, I wanted to feel fulfilled. I really wanted to make a go at this new life but didn't know where to go to start meeting people. After 4-weeks, I joined Avon and, with nothing to lose, dived in headfirst. At first, anxiety tried to talk me out of it; it was trying to protect me, after all. It took such courage to step out the door, but I did it. And again. And again, and again. The more action I took, the easier it became and the more the voice of self-doubt and mind chatter quietened. I couldn't bear the thought of leaving my son in childcare, so he joined me on my rounds, attached to my hip as we knocked door-to-door. This was a huge breakthrough. When once I was too afraid to leave my own home, here I was boldly knocking on the door of complete strangers.

I met so many mums like me who felt lonely and wanted more from life. Avon gave me the flexibility to work around family life while showing them what was possible. Before long, I'd built a team of over 200 reps. I started to feel like me again. I had a purpose. I met some incredible women who have become lifelong friends. Avon set me on a path away from anxiety and towards growth and personal freedom.

It can be challenging to have our needs met when we're not really sure what they are in the first place. What is clear is that our stress, anxiety and behaviours are the perfect signposts for communicating when we are neglecting our needs. How often have you felt lonely so reached for some comfort food or alcohol to meet your need for connection? Has shame been triggered, and you've found yourself reacting as your five-year-old self, acting out and projecting your hurt onto others to meet your need for significance? Perhaps you're irritable or impatient with a loved one in unfamiliar surroundings, such is your need for certainty. Maybe you get bored quickly and lack focus, jumping from one job or relationship to another and internalise this as being a character flaw rather than a strong need for variety.

We all have needs, some with more importance than others. Understanding what they are helps you understand your behaviours (especially some of the unhelpful strategies that can have a detrimental or harmful impact) and is the first step towards discovering who you are.

The Six Human Needs

Six basic human needs drive all human behaviour. Every person on the planet shares the same needs, although we all prioritise them in different ways. How we satisfy those needs is also unique for everyone. For example, the need for variety may be met by travelling for one person while another may fulfil the same need by taking frequent short-term work contracts. The need for connection could be satisfied by chatting to a friend on the phone every day while someone else may meet this need by working in a team instead of as a freelancer working alone from home.

When you know what drives somebody, you're better able to meet their needs. This is useful for partners, children and even work colleagues. Equally, when you understand what drives you, you're more likely to find ways to satisfy your needs instead of seeking ways to meet them on the outside. Your needs will change as you grow. When you review the needs below, you'll find that some will have been stronger in childhood while others may now be surfacing as you're getting older.

Certainty - the need for security, stability, safety, comfort, familiarity and predictability. This can look like staying in the same company for years instead of taking a new job or starting a business.

Variety - the need for adventure, surprise, excitement, a new challenge and change. This can look like changing jobs frequently, going travelling or engaging in high-adrenaline sports.

These two needs work in paradox. If the balance is heavily shifted towards certainty with a lack of variety, then you can feel bored. If the balance weighs heavily on the side of variety, then you may suddenly crave more stability in your life.

Significance - the need to feel needed, wanted, special and important.

Love and Connection - the need for intimacy, attachment, approval and to belong

These two needs are also paradoxes. When we have a high need for significance which is being unmet, we can express unhealthy behaviours such as dominance, control and bullying, and push intimacy - the thing we need to feel significant - away.

Growth - the need for intellectual, emotional, and spiritual development.

Contribution - the need to give, care, protect and serve in ways above and beyond ourselves.

These two needs typically emerge as we get older. They are the needs of the spirit and give a deep sense of happiness and fulfilment.

Exercise: Identify Your Highest Needs

Review the Human Needs. List your needs in order of priority:

1)________________
2) ________________
3) ________________
4) ________________
5) ________________
6) ________________

2) How are you meeting your needs? Are they being met in constructive or destructive ways? If you're meeting your needs externally, how can you pull on your internal resources to ensure that those needs are being met? Take your time to reflect on these questions and don't attach any judgment or guilt to your answers. We are all a work in progress. The more aware you become of your needs and how they are (or are not) being met, the more you take your personal power back and make more positive choices.

What are Your Values?

Our values inform our words, thoughts and actions and help us grow and develop. Quite often we have strong values yet don't live by them. When this happens, we create a sense of unease and discomfort and can feel off balance and out of alignment. This is when stress, anxiety and overwhelm can really take hold. As parents or partners, we may assume that our loved ones share our values and can take it personally when they don't. While it is true that very opposing values can create conflict, it is also true that as individuals we place importance on different things, and that's okay. There's a lot to be said for respecting other people's values, even if they differ to your own.

When you build a life and lifestyle around your values, you create one that is more satisfying and meaningful. You start to do more to align with your values while learning to let go of the things that no longer serve you or bring you joy. You begin to make decisions and more deliberate choices based on your values so that you can move towards the future you want. Values are an excellent tool for finding and developing your inner voice and having the confidence to say no, particular if you're someone who identifies as being a people-pleaser.

Your values change as you evolve and grow. As I found, many of the things that were important to me no longer seemed to matter once my son was born. This is perfectly normal. The important thing is to be tuned in to your values in the present moment and re-evaluate at different life stages if necessary.

See figure 2.1: which of the values jump out you? You'll find that there will be two or three core values that will create a strong almost palpable sensation in your body as you read them.

Figure 2.1 - Values List

Instructions: Your values represent what's important to you in life. Knowing your values helps you understand what drives you, what you enjoy, what inspires you and what you'd like more of.

By building a life & lifestyle around our values we create a life that is satisfying and meaningful to us.

IMPORTANT: Values change over time and deepen as you understand yourself better - they are always moving. Your values can also be situational, e.g. what's true for you at work may not be true for you at home.

Finally, the Sample Values List below is ONLY to give you ideas. We are each unique, so there will undoubtedly be words that are missing from this list, and different words that sum up your values better. Feel free to amend or add to the words in the list below.

1. Accomplishment
2. Accuracy
3. Acknowledgement
4. Adventure
5. Authenticity
6. Balance

34. Focus
35. Forgiveness
36. Freedom
37. Friendship
38. Fun
39. Generosity

67. Presence
68. Productivity
69. Recognition
70. Respect
71. Resourcefulness
72. Romance

7. Beauty
8. Boldness
9. Calm
10. Challenge
11. Collaboration
12. Community
13. Compassion
14. Comradeship
15. Confidence
16. Connectedness
17. Contentment
18. Contribution
19. Cooperation
20. Courage
21. Creativity
22. Curiosity
23. Determination
24. Directness
25. Discovery
26. Ease
27. Effortlessness
28. Empowerment
29. Enthusiasm
30. Environment
31. Excellence
32. Fairness
33. Flexibility
40. Gentleness
41. Growth
42. Happiness
43. Harmony
44. Health
45. Helpfulness
46. Honesty
47. Honour
48. Humour
49. Idealism
50. Independence
51. Innovation
52. Integrity
53. Intuition
54. Joy
55. Kindness
56. Learning
57. Listening
58. Love
59. Loyalty
60. Optimism
61. Orderliness
62. Participation
63. Partnership
64. Passion
65. Patience
66. Peace
73. Safety
74. Self-Esteem
75. Service
76. Simplicity
77. Spaciousness
78. Spirituality
79. Spontaneity
80. Strength
81. Tact
82. Thankfulness
83. Tolerance
84. Tradition
85. Trust
86. Understanding
87. Unity
88. Vitality
89. Wisdom
90. ________________
91. ________________
92. ________________
93. ________________
94. ________________
95. ________________
96. ________________
97. ________________
98. ________________
99. ________________

***Remember**: When it comes to our values, there is no right or wrong - only who WE are!*

Exercise: Identify Your Highest Values

A) What are your top 3 values?

1) ________

2) ________

3) ________

B) Evaluate different areas of your life such as work and relationships. In what ways are you living in alignment with your values? In what ways are you not living in alignment with your values? For the latter, what changes need to be made?

C) Imagine that you're carrying a big, heavy suitcase full of old baggage: old thoughts, expectations, obligations. Observe how much baggage you've been carrying that isn't yours. Visualise yourself emptying the suitcase of old 'stuff' and filling it with your new values and all the things that represent who you are.

"We must accept finite disappointment, but never lose infinite hope."

Martin Luther King Jr.

How Do You See the World?

Ever wondered why there are some people with whom you just don't see eye-to-eye? Perhaps you know some people who are very black and white in their thinking while others can see the grey areas and nuances in between. Maybe you have a vision of a perfect world, devoid of war and conflict, yet see so much separation as you look around you. One thing is for sure - humans are deeply complex beings. We are all here having our own individual experience of life, yet along the way, we forget this. We assume that others should think and feel the way we do and often when they don't, conflict and disagreements arise, especially in our closest relationships.

I grew up thinking that I was never good enough in my mother's eyes. I strived to achieve more to gain her approval yet took her silence, and what I perceived to be disinterest, as a personal failure. Because she never said that she was proud of my achievements I interpreted that as her not caring or even acknowledging me. I questioned her love for me, and our relationship felt strained.

When I did the suitcase exercise from the previous chapter during my coaching training, I visualised taking my people-pleaser and over-giving tendencies out of the suitcase. I realised then that everything I did was to prove myself to my mum. I wanted to please her more than I wanted to please myself. This was a breakthrough moment for me and enabled me to break the pattern and reclaim my power. One day I sat with my mum and opened up about how I felt and how all my life I just wanted her love. Naturally, this was a shock to her. From her perspective, she hadn't seen that she was doing anything wrong. She certainly hadn't intended to cause any upset. Since that conversation we've been able to build a better and stronger relationship as we have a deeper understanding of each other. We respect and accept our differences. We don't always agree on things, yet we can still have a healthy relationship regardless. Because I was so consumed by the lack that I felt and my self-perceived inadequacies, I wasn't able to see my mum's own struggles with anxiety and depression, which she has since opened up about.

The adage 'you don't know what you don't know' is so true in our day-to-day interactions. We form snap judgements about people based on their behaviour, without pausing to consider what is driving it. Perhaps they're experiencing difficulties in their home life or have had some bad news? Maybe someone has crossed a personal boundary, or their beliefs are being challenged? Or, quite simply, they don't see things the same way that we do. The greatest wars are often the ones we have with ourselves. The more storms that brew in our mind, the cloudier our perception of the world and the way we experience it.

Miscommunication, misunderstanding and even conflict occur when we don't respect, acknowledge or empathise with someone else's experience. When we accept the perspective of others, even if we don't agree with them, we can accept our differences and coexist in harmony. True empathy happens when we accept someone else's worldview, even if it differs from our own. But first, we need to understand what shapes our own perception of the world.

How Your Senses Shape How You See the World

We are always aware of what goes on around us through our five senses, even if we are not consciously aware. In each moment we are taking in and processing millions of bits of information through a combination of sight, sound, taste, touch and smell, as well as our sixth sense (intuition). We use our senses as a medium to gather information from outside sources and internalise them using our thoughts. When we are thinking, dreaming, remembering or memorising, we are using these senses internally, which in NLP are known as representational systems or modalities (see figure 3.1).

The five representational systems are:

- The visual system (sight)
- The auditory system (sound)
- The kinaesthetic system (touch/feeling)
- The olfactory system (smell)
- The gustatory system (taste)

These systems give meaning to our experience. We all have the same five representational systems, but each of us differs in the way we represent the world internally. Over time, we generate our own unique way of thinking.

Figure 3.1 – Sub-Modalities

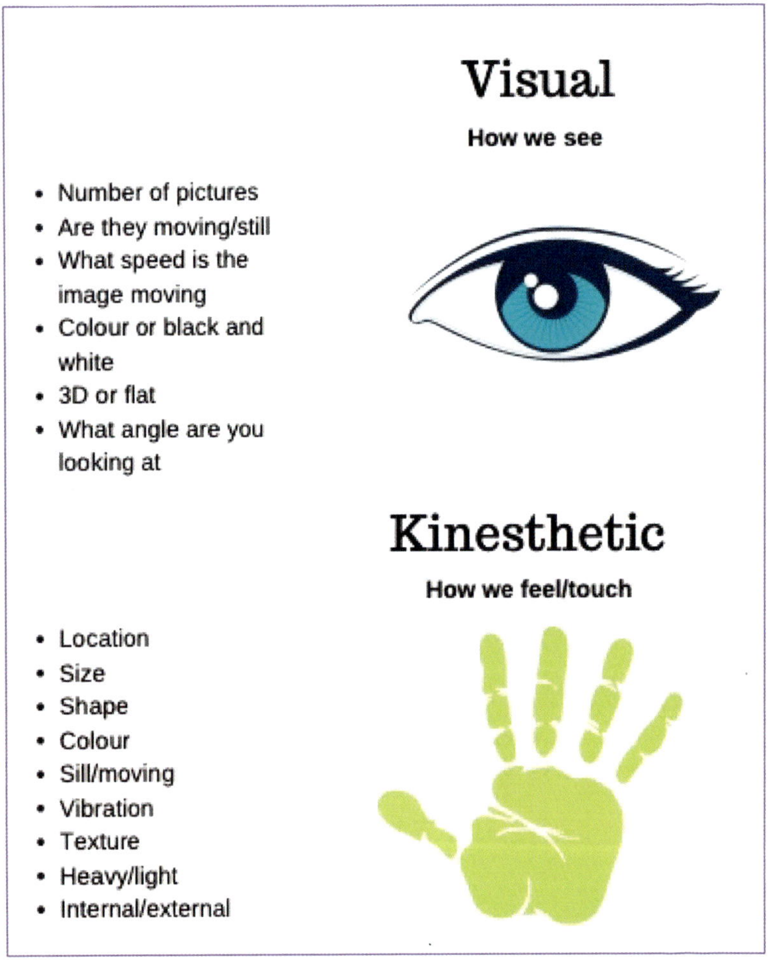

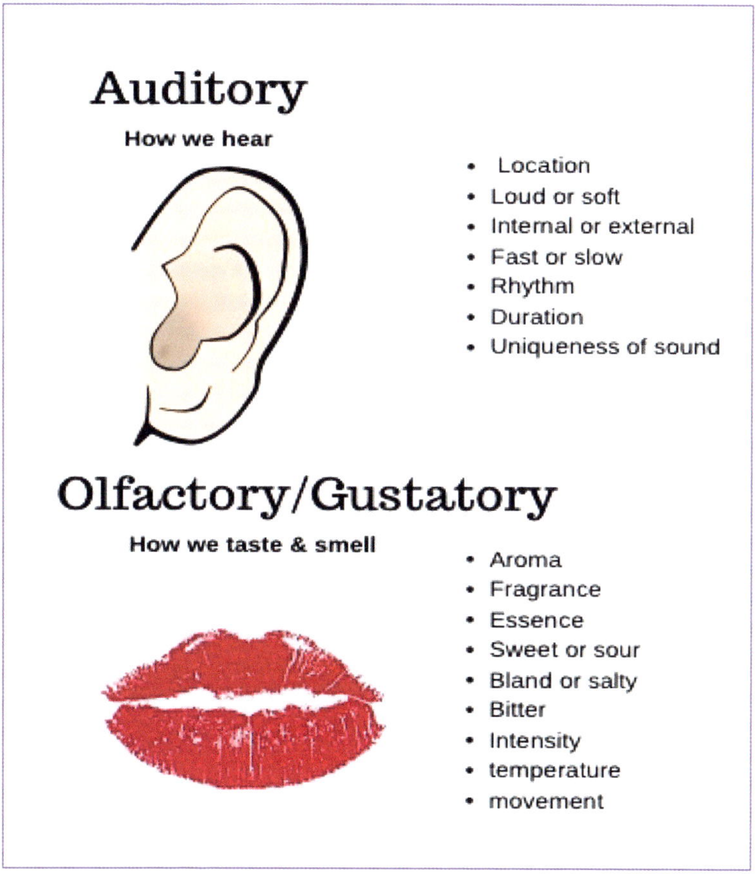

Not surprisingly, the internal pictures, sounds and feelings that every one of us experiences are likely to be different due to our individual subjective interpretations. These differences create different ways of thinking and altered states of mind. For example, we could all watch the same film yet have a completely different opinion or interpretation of it. We can each witness the same event yet have a different feeling and therefore experience of it. Each one of us has a preference for which sense we use to relate to the outer world or to communicate and think. Those who favour images and pictures, or remember faces better rather than sounds, tend to have a primary visual preference. Those who find it easier to remember names, usually through personal introduction (auditory), are likely to have a primary auditory preference. We all unconsciously use all our senses every day though it is typical to have a dominant preference.

Exercise: What do You See?

Take a look at the picture below. What do you first see?

This well-known picture perfectly demonstrates how we can all be look at the same thing yet see something completely different. It also shows that when we shift our perspective and bring new thoughts into our awareness, what we see changes; we start to see what we didn't see before.

Understanding our preferred systems enables us to master our own mind and gain control of how we view external input which can help is in many areas of our lives. When we are learning something new, we can seek out the learning tools and methods that our brain is most likely to assimilate; a visual learner may struggle to learn through audio alone and may prefer video or slides, for example (see figure 3.1 for more about learning styles). When we communicate with our children or partner, we can identify their preferred system and adapt our language for more effective communication.

During times of stress, our senses are heightened. Loud sounds may suddenly become unbearable, or you may find yourself hyper-sensitive to touch and smell. If your preferred system is visual, then light can feel blinding. It's easy to see how, in what can often be a busy and chaotic world, our nervous system can become overloaded, overstimulated and we are left feeling anxious and overwhelmed. When you're starting to feel more sensitive than usual, remember to use the strategies from chapter one to calm your nervous system, or take yourself to a more calming environment, e.g. a walk in nature.

Exercise: VAK Learning Styles Self-Assessment Questionnaire

(with acknowledgements to Victoria Chislett for developing this assessment. Victoria Chislett specialises in performance psychology and its application within organisations and can be contacted via email: performance_psychologist@yahoo.com).

Circle the answers that most represent how you generally behave.

1. When I operate new equipment I generally:
a) read the instructions first
b) listen to an explanation from someone who has used it before
c) go ahead and have a go, I can figure it out as I use it

2. When I need directions for travelling I usually:
a) look at a map
b) ask for spoken directions
c) follow my nose and maybe use a compass

3. When I cook a new dish, I like to:
a) follow a written recipe
b) call a friend for an explanation
c) follow my instincts, testing as I cook

4. If I am teaching someone something new, I tend to:
a) write instructions down for them
b) give them a verbal explanation
c) demonstrate first and then let them have a go

5. I tend to say:
a) watch how I do it
b) listen to me explain
c) you have a go

6. During my free time I most enjoy:

a) going to museums and galleries

b) listening to music and talking to my friends

c) playing a sport or doing DIY

7. When I go shopping for clothes, I tend to:

a) imagine what they would look like on

b) discuss them with the shop staff

c) try them on and test them out

8. When I am choosing a holiday I usually:

a) read lots of brochures

b) listen to recommendations from friends

c) imagine what it would be like to be there

9. If I were buying a new car, I would:

a) read reviews in newspapers and magazines

b) discuss what I need with my friends

c) test-drive lots of different types

10. When I am learning a new skill, I am most comfortable:

a) watching what the teacher is doing

b) talking through with the teacher exactly what I'm supposed to do

c) giving it a try myself and work it out as I go

11. If I am choosing food off a menu, I tend to:

a) imagine what the food will look like

b) talk through the options in my head or with my partner

c) imagine what the food will taste like

12. When I listen to a band, I can't help:

a) watching the band members and other people in the audience

b) listening to the lyrics and the beats

c) moving in time with the music

13. When I concentrate, I most often:

a) focus on the words or the pictures in front of me

b) discuss the problem and the possible solutions in my head

c) move around a lot, fiddle with pens and pencils and touch things

14. I choose household furnishings because I like:

a) their colours and how they look

b) the descriptions the sales-people give me

c) their textures and what it feels like to touch them

15. My first memory is of:

a) looking at something

b) being spoken to

c) doing something

16. When I am anxious, I:

a) visualise the worst-case scenarios

b) talk over in my head what worries me most

c) can't sit still, fiddle and move around constantly

17. I feel especially connected to other people because of:

a) how they look

b) what they say to me

c) how they make me feel

18. When I have to revise for an exam, I generally:

a) write lots of revision notes and diagrams

b) talk over my notes, alone or with other people

c) imagine making the movement or creating the formula

19. If I am explaining to someone I tend to:

a) show them what I mean

b) explain to them in different ways until they understand

c) encourage them to try and talk them through my idea as they do it

20. I really love:

a) watching films, photography, looking at art or people watching

b) listening to music, the radio or talking to friends

c) taking part in sporting activities, eating fine foods and wines or dancing

21. Most of my free time is spent:

a) watching television

b) talking to friends

c) doing physical activity or making things

22. When I first contact a new person, I usually:

a) arrange a face to face meeting

b) talk to them on the telephone

c) try to get together while doing something else, such as an activity or a meal

23. I first notice how people:

a) look and dress

b) sound and speak

c) stand and move

24. If I am angry, I tend to:

a) keep replaying in my mind what it is that has upset me

b) raise my voice and tell people how I feel

c) stamp about, slam doors and physically demonstrate my anger

25. I find it easier to remember:

a) faces

b) names

c) things I have done

26. I think that you can tell if someone is lying if:

a) they avoid looking at you

b) their voice changes

c) they give me funny vibes

27. When I meet an old friend:

a) I say, 'it's great to see you!'

b) I say, 'it's great to hear from you!'

c) I give them a hug or a handshake

28. I remember things best by:

a) writing notes or keeping printed details

b) saying them aloud or repeating words and key points in my head

c) doing and practising the activity or imagining it being done

29. If I have to complain about faulty goods, I am most comfortable:

a) writing a letter

b) complaining over the phone

c) taking the item back to the store or posting it to head office

30. I tend to say:

a) I see what you mean

b) I hear what you are saying

c) I know how you feel

Now add up how many A's, B's and C's you selected.

If you chose mostly A's, you have a VISUAL learning style.
If you chose mostly B's, you have an AUDITORY learning style.
If you chose mostly C's, you have a KINESTHETIC learning style.

Someone with a **Visual** learning style has a preference for seen or observed things, including pictures, diagrams, demonstrations, displays, handouts, films, flip-charts, etc. These people will use phrases such as 'show me', and 'let's take a look at that,' and will be best able to perform a new task after reading the instructions or watching someone else do it first. Their eyes will likely move to the top left or right when they are recalling a memory or constructing a new visual representation. These are the people who will work from lists and written directions and instructions.

Someone with an **Auditory** learning style has a preference for the transfer of information through listening: to the spoken word, of self or others, of sounds and noises. These people will use phrases such as 'tell me', and 'let's talk it over,' and will be best able to perform a new task after listening to instructions from an expert. These are the people who are happy being given spoken instructions over the telephone and can remember all the words to songs that they hear! Those locating information auditorily will have a tendency to look middle left (constructed) or middle right (memory).

Someone with a **Kinaesthetic** learning style has a preference for physical experience -touching, feeling, holding, doing, practical hands-on experiences. These people will use phrases such as 'let me try', and 'how do you feel?' and will be best able to perform a new task by going ahead and trying it out, learning as they go. These are the people who like to experiment, hands-on, and never look at the instructions first! Those locating information kinaesthetically will have a tendency to look to the lower left when they are recalling information. Self-Talk or calculation occur when looking to the lower right; you will know when someone is experiencing shame because this is where they will look when their negative self-talk kicks in.

When you know your preferred learning style(s), you understand the type of learning that best suits you, enabling you to choose the types of learning that work best for you. It's also a useful tool to help you communicate more effectively. When you can identify the preferred learning style of others, you can adapt your language and the way you deliver your message for better understanding.

How We Filter the World Using Our Five Senses

Nearly eight billion people are living on this planet right now. That's eight billion people with different experiences, beliefs and filters that create their unique view of the world. No two people will see the world in precisely the same way. Even if one hundred people were looking at the same wall, they only see that wall through their own eyes and with their own senses, i.e. from their own unique perspective. Beliefs, attitudes, and values may be shared but each person is different and how information is processed, stored and filtered varies. How we experience emotion differs too. While the feeling itself is generally the same, the catalyst can be different. We all know what sadness feels like, yet we may not feel sad about the same things. People respond to their 'map' of reality, not to reality itself, meaning that each individual's perception of an event is different.

The NLP Communication Model, developed by Tad James & Wyatt Woodsmall (1988) from the work of Richard Bandler & John Grinder (1975), explains how we take information from the outside world, how we process and filter it, and how it affects our thoughts, feelings and behaviour.

Every second of every day we are exposed to millions of bits of information in the environment around us which we process through our five senses - sight, sound, smell, touch and taste. Most of this information is absorbed and assimilated unconsciously, our nervous system filtering the relevant information from the not-so-relevant.

Mind filtering is a wonderful subject to understand and explore. The way I filter information versus someone else will be completely different. I may delete the data, distort it or make assumptions, depending on my values, attitudes and belief system. It's easy to see how a breakdown in communication can occur when one person makes assumptions while the other is left feeling unheard. It's also easy to see how, when there are shared beliefs, e.g. religion we are more likely to build a rapport with someone and accept the information as truth, without challenging it. Likewise, we can often too-readily dismiss the information, and delete it altogether, when it isn't aligned to our own view of the world.

Leanne came to me very quiet, anxious and had very little belief in herself and no sense of direction, purpose or clarity. After our six-week course Leanne now stands tall and has a purpose. Leanne is now focussed on her future and set goals and gained so much confidence.

" In a short amount of time, I have gone from being quite a timid and anxious person, to someone with a lot of happiness and confidence. I know where I want to be in life thanks to Hayley!"
- Leanne Brown

Figure 3.2: Mind Map – How We View the World

Our individual filters are primarily determined by the beliefs, values and attitudes we adopted from our childhood plus the relationships and experiences we were exposed to. The language we use, our understanding of words and gestures, and our memories (conscious and unconscious) also play a part.

We then delete, distort or make assumptions according to our unique filters. Our internal map of reality is created by the thoughts constructed from filtered information. These maps (or internal representations) take the form of sensory perceptions which creates our in-the-moment experience: a picture with sounds, emotions, tastes and smells. Our map of reality can trigger other states which then motivate our behaviour. If something triggers an unwanted state, this can lead to unwanted behaviour.

My map of reality was based on assumptions I'd made about my mum not caring about me causing me to seek evidence to confirm this belief and create a self-fulfilling prophecy. The feeling around this triggered an anxious state and perfectionist and controlling behaviours. Our map (or view) of reality determines how we view the world and everything we experience in it.

As mentioned, we do at least one of three things with filtered information. We either delete, distort, make assumptions, or do a combination of each.

Deletion – Every day our nervous system is exposed to billions of bits of information, far too much for our brain to absorb, assimilate or get any use out of. In a nano-second, your brain will unconsciously omit certain information by selecting bits of it that it deems most important. It's one of the reasons why ten people could give a completely different account of the same event because their brain has selected specific snippets of information over others. Again, your values, beliefs and attitudes will determine the pieces of information that you consider to be most important. If you imagine editing a book or a blog post, for example, you would remove any irrelevant text. This is what your brain does, albeit so fast you don't even notice or have any conscious awareness of it!

Distortion - we distort information all the time. Perhaps you've had a conversation with someone and completely misinterpreted what they said. Maybe you feel intimidated by certain people for no other reason than the stories and judgements you've created in your mind. Over time memories can become distorted and you can start doubting your version of events. Distortion can be positive too. Planning and visualising, for example, can help construct future goals and outcomes by re-wiring the brain (creating new connections).

Assumptions - we make assumptions all the time, rightly or wrongly. Assumptions are the conclusions we draw based upon experience or the information we have at the time. Sometimes we might make assumptions about another person's behaviour based on what knowledge we have of that person, or how we have experienced similar behaviours up until that point. When we're growing and learning, we make assumptions about how things will work based on what we have already learned, e.g. knowing that a door will open when you turn the handle because that's been your experience of a door. Negative experiences can result in negative assumptions, e.g. falling into a pool as a child could lead to a fear of water later on in life, or having a negative experience of an adult male could lead to assuming that all men are bad.

Many relationships break down because of poor communication and misunderstanding. When we understand the NLP Communication Model and the various factors that create our view of the world and how this can impact our communication, we can become more compassionate, not only with ourselves but for others too. We can stop fighting the need to be right, and instead, better understand and respect other people's points of view. We become more active listeners and relate to people better, meeting them where they're at and responding appropriately. This facilitates empathy as we recognise that everyone's experience is real and valid, even if it differs from our own.

The good news is that our brains can be re-wired for success. With awareness and the use of NLP techniques, we can gain control of our internal processes and therefore change our behaviours and the way we communicate. We can become less affected by external circumstances, shifting from reactivity to a calmer, more measured response, and be more conscious in our interactions with others. My mum and I have different maps of reality, but this doesn't stop our relationship going from strength-to-strength. The clearer we communicate, regardless of whether we're in agreement or not, the less room there is for misunderstanding.

Human Behaviour

In chapter two we spoke about the six human needs and values that drive human behaviour. When we recognise the ways we do or don't meet our own needs, we're better able to understand our behaviour. Likewise, when we can observe that the behaviour of others is driven by their needs, we can show more understanding during times of negative behaviour.

Many of us have been raised in what has primarily been a behavioural-focused society. Schools and parents have used reward and punishment to correct unwanted behaviour for generations. As a result, our brains have been wired to seek reward and validation, exacerbating anxiety, while also internalising a lot of fear. When we can see negative behaviour as being communication - an expression of an unmet need or a reaction to fear and anxiety - we can remedy it at its source, rather than trying to 'fix' the symptom. Because we are only ever seeing the world through our own eyes and based on our own internal representation, we can become very judgemental towards others, especially if they behave in a way that challenges our personal values, beliefs or even level of developmental maturity. This is particularly true when we parent our own children.

Very few people intend to cause harm to others. Of course, we can find examples where harm is inflicted with very deliberate intent; however, most of us are doing our best with our thoughts and feelings moment to moment. For some of us, that means responding more calmly, while for others it means falling into reactivity, depending on our level of stress and anxiety at the time. As the adage goes, hurt people hurt people; someone's internal pain and suffering can very quickly be projected onto others. Even some of the worse behaviour has positive intent behind it when we look beneath the behaviour and see the different layers and filtering that have shaped a person's world view. Morality aside, what is considered 'good' or 'bad' behaviour is very subjective.

Empathy is recognising, acknowledging and accepting someone else's experience, even when it differs from our own or is something we can't make sense of. Everybody's experience is valid and real. What may seem irrational to one person is very real and rational to someone else. When we're anxious, the threat may not be real, but the thoughts have us believe that it is. And, as we discovered when we looked at stress and anxiety in chapter one, anxious thoughts can lead to unwanted behaviours. No one truly knows what someone else is experiencing unless they're walking in their shoes (which none of us can; we can only walk in our own).

* If you find yourself judging others for their behaviour, remind yourself that they're having their own experience. Recognise that in most people's mind is a battlefield, not always seen on the outside.

* If you're being too hard on yourself, show yourself some compassion. We all make mistakes and do what makes sense at the time, even if in hindsight it was a bad idea.

* If you find yourself in conflict with someone, recognise that it is a conflict of two world views. Neither is right or wrong, merely personal and unique to you. Instead of defending your world view, get curious about theirs.

* Be more open to listening to someone else's perspective, without pointing the finger of blame or shame. Being human isn't always easy; we're all here to learn.

Exercise: Active Listening

Find a partner and invite them to share something with you, e.g. a problem, a story, something they need to get clarity on. Set a timer and allow them to speak for 10-minutes. Your role here is to listen and only listen without saying a word. When the time is up, spend two minutes reflecting back to them what you heard.

Was there anything you heard beyond the words, i.e. they didn't articulate it, but you heard it and felt it?

Were there times you wanted to jump in and respond? Maybe they started crying and you felt the need to comfort or 'fix' them? Perhaps mentally you took notes of what to say, or were thinking of your own anecdotes to centre yourself in the conversation. Did your mind wander or were your present? Observe your own role as a listener without judgement.

On a scale of 1-10 (10 being the highest), how comfortable did you feel listening without being able to speak?

Now swap roles: you speak, the other person listens. Talk for 10-minutes about anything that is on your mind. As before, when the time is up, the listener spends 2-minutes reflecting back what they heard.

How was your experience as the speaker? How did it feel to have someone holding space for you? Perhaps you felt the other person was distracted – how did that feel?

How did it feel to be in both roles? Was there anything you felt about your connection with the other person?

Many of us have been conditioned to rescue others or take their pain away, especially in very co-dependent relationships. When listening, never underestimate the healing power of silence!

The **presuppositions of NLP** are a set of guiding principles to live by that can be used as a reminder to show more compassion, kindness and empathy towards others:

- Have respect for the other person's model of the world.
- We are all unique and experience the world in different ways. Everyone is an individual and has their own unique way of being.
- The map is not the territory.
- People respond to their 'map' of reality, not to reality itself. How people make sense of the world around them is through their senses and from their own personal experience; this means that each individual's perception of an event is different.
- Mind and body form a linked system.
- Your mental attitude affects your body and your health and, in turn, how you behave.
- If what you are doing isn't working, do something else.
- Flexibility is the key to success.
- Choice is better than no choice.
- Having options can provide more opportunities for achieving results.

- We are always communicating.

- Even when we remain silent, we are communicating. Non-verbal communication can account for a large proportion of a message.

- The meaning of your communication is the response you get.

- While your intention may be clear to you, it is the other person's interpretation and response that reflects your effectiveness. NLP teaches you the skills and flexibility to ensure that the message you send equals the message they receive.

- There is no failure, only feedback.

- What seemed like failure can be thought of as success that just stopped too soon. With this understanding, we can stop blaming ourselves and others, find solutions and improve the quality of what we do.

- Behind every behaviour, there is a positive intention.

- When we understand that other people have some positive intention in what they say and do (however annoying and negative it may seem to us), it can be easier to stop getting angry and start to move forward.

Steve came to work with me and was very depressed. Steve has sadly lost one of his children who died at such a young age. He had also been mentally abused by his ex and had no self-love, value or belief. Steve was at a loss and didn't even think about a future. After our sessions I am pleased to say that it's been very emotional, he has let go of so much hurt and baggage. Steve has created new values and beliefs and has learnt coping skills. Steve is now ready for work and keen to get back out into the community again. I am proud that he has been volunteering and now understands his worth and has self-belief. Finally, Steve can see a future.

"After my life took one too many kicks and wrong turns, I was in a state of flux, couldn't see a future, didn't have the ambition and drive to even think about creating one... I was an angry, trod upon, misunderstood, abject failure... or so I thought. I was referred to Hayley and entered a six-week course. I may still be overweight, currently out of work and losing hair but the pure positivity that Hayley exudes through her coaching sessions has brought me to the point where I AM looking at a future and have the renewed confidence to Achieve again. She has made me believe in myself through my previous mistakes and failures and made me realise that the Past is exactly that. She has given me simple tools and methods to cope with life's ups and downs and I have now re-boarded the Rollercoaster in the front carriage with a smile and both arms in the air".

- S. McGrath

"A mother who radiates self-acceptance actually vaccinates her daughter against low self-esteem"

Naomi Wolf

Developing a Growth Mindset (and Rewiring Your Brain)

Until relatively recently, it was believed that the brain was 'plastic' meaning that it was fixed; you were only as good as the brain you were born with. This impacted the way we understood learning and what it takes to be successful: you were either intelligent, or not; you either had a natural aptitude for something, or you didn't. Many a child has been left on the 'scrapheap', believing that they're good for nothing because of their lack of mental ability and intelligence, diminishing their self-esteem and creating a self-fulfilling prophecy based upon their limitations. Thanks to recent advances in neuroscience and the work of Carol Dweck, we now know that the brain is far more malleable than we first thought.

Since the discovery of neuroplasticity, we now know that our experiences change the physical structure of our brain. With practice, neural pathways grow new connections and strengthen existing ones. These neuroscientific discoveries have shown us that we can increase our neural growth by the actions we take, such as using good strategies, journaling, asking questions, practising consistently, and evening adding a gratitude practice into your daily routine. Instead of giving up when things feel hard, or not even trying because of our limiting beliefs, we open the possibilities of what can be achieved, regardless of natural ability or traits. We're no longer confined by how our brain works right now; we can re-shape and re-wire our brains to live healthier, happier and more successful lives.

Developing a growth mindset is especially important for those struggling with anxiety. When our mindset is fixed, we fear making mistakes, thus triggering our stress response. If we're too afraid to make mistakes because we fear the consequences - and loss of control that comes with an anxious state - we hold ourselves back, play small and avoid taking risks. We try to control the outcome and struggle to deviate or be flexible. We put added pressure on ourselves to perform well and do things the 'right' way. This is very limiting to our overall sense of happiness, wellbeing and life success.

Rewarding or praising an outcome rather than progress is a contributing factor for having a fixed mindset. Many of us were raised and educated where rewards and punishments were used to control and correct behaviour. We now have evidence to show that praising effort and progress helps to cultivate a growth mindset. Shifting from a fixed to growth mindset has been proven to lead to increased motivation, self-belief and achievement. Those with a fixed mindset tend to be 'set in their ways' and more resistant to change, while those with a growth mindset are more flexible, embrace change, focus on solutions not problems, and are better equipped to navigate life's challenges.

Dialogue for a Growth Mindset in Children

'You/I can't do it...yet!'

'What can you learn from this mistake?'

'Keep trying, it'll be worth it.'

'That's an amazing piece of work...how long did it take you?'

'Every time something feels hard, you're giving your brain an excellent work-out so it can stretch and learn.'

'Everyone learns in different ways. Let's find a way that suits you.'

'Well done! Look what you can do when you work hard and put in the effort.'

'That's a great painting ... tell me about the process.'

'It's great being bored. I wonder what brilliant ideas will pop into your head.'

'You've really improved because you've been putting in the effort.'

'It's great that you asked for help. It shows how you're willing to learn.'

'I've noticed you putting in a lot of practice....and look how much easier it's getting.'

Journaling

Journaling is a powerful way to gain clarity, release stuck emotions, bring unconscious patterns into your awareness, access your intuition and fire new connections in your brain. Keeping a journal is a great way to build better habits, as it forces you to be aware of your actions and behaviours.

Your journal has the potential to be a therapist, friend and coach, who listens without judging and is available 24 hours a day. You can verbalise your thoughts in writing to help you better understand what you're feeling, freeing up thinking space to gain clarity on what to do next. When we journal from a really grounded place and let the words flow freely, we can access our intuition and use our wisdom to guide us. When we journal on a future vision, the act of writing brings our vision into the present moment and fires our brain cells and grow new connections as we start to take action towards it.

By consciously looking back over your journals, you're able to track progress and patterns of behaviour that help you achieve goals, as well as those that get in the way of personal and professional growth. By becoming mindful with what you are discovering, you can move from knowing into a doing state.

Because you're in dialogue with your inner self, journaling enables you to solve problems and get creative. Journals give voice to your dreams and aspirations and are also safe spaces to release the negative emotions that could get in the way of them.

If you want to unravel the workings of your inner world and the patterns buried in the depths of your psyche, free-flow writing is the most potent form of journaling. This is best done first thing in the morning, upon waking, when you're in a theta state. Spend some time in stillness - meditate if you need to - then begin by writing a prompt on the paper. Let your hand move freely as the words start to flow and a stream of consciousness spills out onto the paper. Make a point of re-reading your journals every few months. You'll be surprised at how much of what is in your journals has become your reality.

Example journaling prompts:

What do I need to know today...?

What do I need to know about...?

To achieve [insert goal] the person I need to be is...

When I achieve [insert goal] I will feel...

Why am I here...?

What is my purpose/mission...?

Why do I feel____about_____?

My deepest desire is...

Today on the [insert a future date] I have achieved...

Journaling can also be used more consciously as a tool for reflection and to track your progress. At the end of each day, pull out your journal and follow the prompts below:

- Write down your top 3 successes today.
- Have you learned something new today? What have you learned about yourself? Who inspired you? Who or what challenged you?
- What did you do to look after yourself today?
- What actions, thoughts or steps did you take today to move you towards your goals or aspirations?

Practise Gratitude

'Cultivate the habit of being grateful for every good thing that comes to you, and to give thanks continuously. And because all things have contributed to your advancement, you should include all things in your gratitude.' — Ralph Waldo Emerson

Gratitude is a deeper appreciation for someone (or something) which produces longer lasting positivity. The Harvard Medical School describes gratitude as 'a thankful appreciation for what an individual receives, whether tangible or intangible. With gratitude, people acknowledge the goodness in their lives ... As a result, gratitude also helps people connect to something larger than themselves as individuals – whether to other people, nature, or a higher power.'

In a state of gratitude, we say yes to life. We affirm that life is good and worth living - even when our circumstances may suggest otherwise. Simply being grateful for being alive is a great way to motivate oneself to seize the day. For some, the idea that tomorrow is not guaranteed is a strong motivator.

Physiologically, shifting into gratitude can calm our nervous system and move us from a stressed to a relaxed state. Focusing on all that we are grateful for can change a negative mindset to a positive one, and away from anxious thinking.

Here are four benefits of expressing gratitude:

1) Gratitude shifts your focus. Life is all about focus. Whatever we focus on, we move towards. When we live in a state of lack, scarcity and negativity, more of it comes into our awareness. It's easy to see all the problems and drama surrounding a situation when your thinking is habitually geared towards that. Likewise, when you focus on the positive, it's easier to see things in a positive light, even when problems arise.

2) Gratitude improves the quality of your life. Gratitude can change your life simply by improving the quality of it. You're the sum of all your parts - physically, spiritually, mentally and emotionally - and gratitude benefits each of those small parts.

3) Gratitude reduces your innermost fears. It's hard to be fearful and grateful at the same time. Fear occurs when we dwell on things that we cannot control. By being grateful, fear can be overcome. When we're thankful for all that we have, including our problems, fear has little space to live in our minds.

4) Gratitude encourages you to reach for your goals. When you set goals, you can achieve anything you put your mind to through consistent and persistent action. Gratitude helps you to succeed by first creating a platform for internal success. When you're happy, healthy and physically, emotionally and spiritually well, you can reach for your goals without little external distraction. When you're unhappy, you live in a state of negativity and lack, and it's harder to push forward.

Exercise: Gratitude Journaling

Keep a gratitude journal. Every night before bed, write a list of 10 to 20 things to feel grateful for. Notice how shifting into a space of gratitude and appreciation can lift your mood and create a sense of inner peace.

Exercise 2: Practice Daily Gratitude

Use the template as a guide to practise gratitude on a daily basis, until it becomes second nature!

Practicing Daily Gratitude

Pat yourself on the back

What did you do today that required a positive choice

My Progress & Success Today

(3 things you have had success or progress with today)

1.
2.
3.

What have you learned from today?

What if anything triggered me today?

Where do i need to be kinder to myself?

Grattitude & Appreciation

(3 things you are grateful or appreciate)

1.
2.
3.

HOW WAS MY DAY? THE SCORE FOR MY DAY IS............../ 10

Sam Tissington has been a joy to work with. Sam at the beginning was very sceptical and worried about the process. After our first session, he went away feeling very excited. Sam suffered from self-belief, and negative thoughts and didn't know who he was anymore. Sam over ate and had poor sleep and diet. Sam is now eating healthy by cutting out convenience foods, found a hobby and started looking for work. His self-confidence is now beaming!

"Working with Hayley has been the best thing I have did. I went in there sceptical but willing to try anything. After my first session I knew this was for me. We discussed in detail all that I was unhappy with in my life, and how we could fix these. We started with simple things, like how I spoke and the negative words I used could affect me. By changing these small things, I noticed a positive change within days. The first hypnotherapy session I had was amazing. The work Hayley did with me was very subtle, I genuinely thought it hadn't worked, until a few hours later and I noticed my thinking, attitude and outlook was positive and focused. These sessions continued reinforcing all he good and positive and about myself, and with just a few changes here and there, changing my negatives into positives. I have never been more driven to achieve my goals; my mental health has never been so good, and this is all down to Hayley and her incredible work. I couldn't possibly recommend (or thank) her enough"

- Sam Tissington

"The greatest source of happiness is the ability to be grateful at all times."

Zig Ziglar

Finding Your Life Purpose

Searching for our purpose can leave many of us stuck and stumbling through life. As we grow, it's not uncommon to seek more meaning and understanding of why we are here and where we fit into the world, especially when our needs shift towards growth and contribution. The truth is, we are all here for more than we realise and while we are continually evolving, our purpose changes over time too. The good news is we are surrounded by clues and nudges pointing us towards our purpose. We need only pay attention!

I loved my Avon business yet had an empty, nagging feeling inside. Something was missing; a part of me wouldn't settle and wanted more. While my business was a success, I didn't feel fulfilled. Avon ticked all the boxes, I had an incredible team, I'd won awards, and my anxiety had all but become a thing of the past. Yet a gaping hole was opening up. I wanted to give more in a bigger way and make a more significant impact, but I was at a loss as to which direction to take.

One of my team leaders suffered from PTSD. I would speak to her daily to help talk her through her fears and anxiety. She was raised with a drug dealer and had an abusive and neglectful upbringing with little further education and zero self-belief. She saw Avon as a chance to make something of herself, but her past haunted her and held her back. Through regular contact and mentoring she won a five-star holiday and was able to create a life and home that she never had. 'You'd be really good at helping people,' she said to me one day. Other team members suggested I become a coach, which had been a natural part of my team building anyway.

I became curious and researched life coaching. Soon I stumbled upon Mark Shields who offered NLP training with the UK Life Practice Academy in Hitchin. Something resonated and I had an overwhelming urge to train with him and become an accredited NLP Life Transformation Coach. I took the leap, and one year later I was qualified.

During my training, I learnt an incredible amount about myself. As much as it was about learning the tools and techniques to help others, it also took me on a personal journey of self-discovery. I realised that my entire life I had pushed myself to succeed for my mum's approval, not for my own. This was a huge lightbulb moment for me, and with that realisation, I was able to start reclaiming my power and connecting with my own inner voice.

We all have an inner voice, one that can be pretty harsh and is often born from the criticism we experienced throughout childhood, while the other is wiser and leads us in the direction of our purpose and potential. Unfortunately, our harsh inner critic often rules the show, so the other is often ignored. However, when we start to pay attention and listen to our inner guidance, it often leads us towards a more meaningful path. Sometimes a common theme will spring into our awareness, or we notice the things that we become hugely passionate about. For me, my NLP training unlocked a deep desire to help others with the very issues I had experienced. It was almost as if my life had left bread crumbs which lead me exactly to where I needed to be. When I thought about helping others with stress and anxiety, something inside radically shifted. I felt alive. This was what I was meant to do with my life! I knew it was my destiny. My inner critic didn't even have a bad word to say. From that moment my coaching business was born. I now run two businesses - Avon and coaching - and I finally feel complete. There is no better feeling than helping others develop to become the best version of themselves.

Life as it is Now

We're all guilty of complaining about certain aspects of our lives – work, health, relationships and finances – yet seldom do we do anything about it. Despite the best of our intentions and our resolve to change, life gets in the way and we fall into our usual patterns and routines. When our reality doesn't match the fantasy of how we think our lives 'should' be, we're left feeling disappointed, despondent and apathetic. We may feel that life is happening 'to' us and that we don't deserve to be happy. We may believe that change is out of our control and that we should accept the hand that we've been dealt. With shiny Insta-worthy photos clogging our social media timelines, we assume that everyone else is happier and living a better life; we cannot resist comparing ourselves to the huge grins, happy families, perfect bodies and the people we perceive as having it all. Comparisonitis is not good for anxiety!

With our minds future focused and thinking about a time when we will be happy e.g. when we are rich, or lose weight, or find the partner of our dreams, we're taken away from the present moment and our levels of anxiety increase. Little wonder that we struggle to know who we are or what we truly want in life.

Before you dive into living a more purposeful and passion-filled life, it helps to evaluate where you're at in your life right now. This gives you a starting point for where you want to go. Accepting your life in its current state is the first step. This doesn't mean that you have to tolerate your life and continue to allow it to be this way. On the contrary, by accepting where you are now brings you back into the present and enables you to effect change from a more grounded and embodied place. The truth is, we all have so much to be grateful for, even if it feels that life is delivering blow after blow. Expressing gratitude for all that we have, including difficult relationships or mounting debt, can shift us into a place of acceptance and appreciation, from which we can create a more authentic vision for the future, instead of one created from a place of lack or fear.

We all have the power within us to effect change. We are inbuilt for insight, our ability to glean clarity even in the foggiest of moments, a system to guide us in difficult times should we choose to listen. We're all more resilient than we give ourselves credit for. Everything we need is already within us; sometimes we just need a little help along the way.

Exercise: Where You Are Now

Using the table on the following page, take some time to reflect on the different areas of your life and score them accordingly. Maybe you've never expressed how you really feel, and this is the first time that you're getting it out of your head, making it more real. If this sounds like you, use this as an opportunity to be honest with yourself. Detach from judgement or feelings of guilt; it's okay to feel dissatisfied and to want more from life. You don't have to share your result with anybody, but you can use it as motivation to create change, no matter how small. Revisit this exercise several times a year so that you can reflect on how far you've come, and the areas you need to improve on.

Laurence came to me with severe anxiety and didn't value himself. After a 6-week course Laurence has moved forwards with new goals, values and has lots of confidence. He can control his anxieties, relaxes well and is taking the next steps to achieve his career goals.

"I have suffered from depression and anxiety over the last 4 years with this increasing in severity over the last 12 months. When I met Hayley, I felt anxious constantly and was unable to sleep and relax. I also didn't value myself or my relationships in the way that I should. Now I feel inspired, positive & empowered by the changes Hayley has helped me to implement within my life"

- Laurence Motley

THE FOUR AREAS OF LIFE STYLE

Please score each area out of 50. Total score 200.
For example: control = 8 approval =5 and so on
*Take Sleep, Caffeine, Alcohol, Tobacco , Exercise and Diet into consideration when scoring

CAREER	HEALTH
Control approval security purpose achievement	Control approval security purpose achievement
FINANCES	**RELATIONSHIPS**
Control approval security purpose achievement	Control approval security purpose achievement

*Marks out of 50 for Career, Health, Finances and Relationship. Please mark in the boxes.

Hayley Austin

Exercise: Where You Want to Go

A swot analysis is an important step to finding personal and career direction. This is a great exercise to do to get clear on the specific areas needing change or improvement. The idea here is not to be self-critical. The questions are to be answered honestly and objectively, thinking about what others around you may say about you. Be positive!

STRENTHGS

What are your strengths?
What do others see your strengths as?
What are your skills?
What are you proud of?

WEEKNESS

What could you do better?
What do you avoid?
What do others see as your weakness?
What do you need to do to face up?

OPPORTUNITIES

What opportunities are out there for you?
What trends can you take advantage of?
What strengths can you turn into opportunities?
Is there anyone you can collaborate with?

THREATS

What trends and threats could harm you?
What is your competition doing?
What obstacles do you have coming up?
Have you allocated yourself enough time?

Living a Passion-filled Life

Most of us have no clue what we want to do with our lives, even after we've ticked all the boxes - the grades, the job, the money, the 2.4 children. Chances are if you're anything like I was, you have no clue what you want to do. It's a struggle almost every adult goes through. 'What do I want to do with my life?' 'What am I passionate about?' 'What am I good at?' are the questions that often plague us.

Part of the problem is the concept of 'life purpose' itself. We're often told that we were each born for some higher purpose and it's now our cosmic mission to find it. While it is true we are here for me than plodding our way through life, there isn't one single purpose. What you feel called to and what you consider important will change over time. The first step, therefore, is to let go of the idea that there is only one purpose for you and embrace the idea that our purpose in life is to love and live life fully.

Here's the truth. We exist on this earth for an undetermined period. During that time, we do things. Some of these things are important while others are unimportant. The important things give our lives meaning and happiness. The unimportant ones basically just kill time. When people say, 'What should I do with my life?' or 'What is my life purpose?' what they're actually asking is: 'What can I do with my time that is important?'

If you reflect on your life, you will recognise the times when your passions have ebbed and flowed. Perhaps one year you invested all your time and energy into learning a musical instrument then the following year you reached your peak, lost interest and moved onto something new. It's unusual for a single passion or enthusiasm to stay exclusively with us for a lifetime, which is why it's pretty unrealistic to expect school leavers to know what they want to do with their lives. The reality is that many of us are multi-passionate. What is important to you today may change next year or even tomorrow, and that's okay. What's crucial is honouring where you're at now and following your passion at this moment. If you want to live and engage in life fully, follow your passions, moment to moment. When we live a passion-filled life, we are living on purpose, and that is the real purpose of life.

If you're feeling stuck and struggling to move forward, reflect on the questions in the exercise below. Grab a pen and journal if you need to.

Exercise: Finding Your Passion Part I

1. What struggle or sacrifice are you willing to tolerate? Ultimately our 'why' determines our ability to keep moving forward and stick with it through the good and bad days. Can you handle rejection and failure?

2. What is true about you today? We all lose touch with what we enjoyed doing as a child. We were taught only to get jobs done in exchange for a reward, so learned to favour results and external gain over our intrinsic learning and passion and joy. What would the childlike version of you say about you today?

3. What is your passion? It's easy to get sucked into society and work until retirement on only a small percentage of earnings. It's not until a light switches on inside of us that we realise what our passion is. What are the things that light you up and excite you? What do you like doing that you could make a living from?

4. How are you going to make an impact? Find a problem you care about and start solving it. Obviously, you're not going to fix the world's problems by yourself. But you can contribute and make a difference. And that feeling of making a difference will ultimately lead to happiness and fulfilment.

5. If you had one year to live, what would you do? How would you utilise your time? What is your legacy going to be? What are the stories people are going to tell when you're gone? What is your obituary going to say? Is there anything to say at all? If not, what would you like it to say? How can you start working towards that today?

6. Do you know who you really are? Who would you be without all the labels? What are your deepest unexpressed desires? What are your dreams? Strip yourself bare and go on a journey of self-discovery. You may be surprised by what you learn about yourself.

Exercise: Find Your Passion Part 2

Using the venn diagram below as a guide, draw four overlapping empty circles on a piece of paper and make notes in each of the sections (as per below). The star in the middle is your sweet spot!

Goal Setting

Modern life is fast-paced, anxiety-inducing and full of shiny objects and obstacles to distract us from our purpose. Even when we are clear on our mission, we can quickly lose sight and get stuck on a hamster wheel, struggling to get off. To remain focused, it is useful to set realistic and manageable goals.

Goal setting is a great strategy to help you work out what you really want, motivate you and keep you focused on the big picture, so you don't lose direction. It gives you a plan of action to achieve your dreams. Since your goals will be personal and meaningful to you and based on what you really want, you will be motivated to achieve them. Goal setting will help you focus your time and energy in the right direction.

Goals are well-defined targets that give you direction and motivation. They are your roadmap to success (whatever that looks like for you), your life's plan and your personal guide to the future.

Goals can be focused on:

Developing a new skill – perhaps you've always wanted to learn a new language, how to dance or play a musical instrument.

Improving your current skills, whether they are focused on career tasks or life skills such as budgeting.

Beating old habits like smoking or developing healthier ones like exercise and healthy eating.

Producing an outcome and achieving your dream – it could be creating more harmonious relationships with your family, wealth creation or achieving a career goal.

As with your passions and purpose, goals will change over time. That's why it's seldom useful to pull together a five-year plan, for example; we just don't know who we're going to be and the ways that we'll change in the future.

The most important thing to remember is that goals are personal – they are yours and yours alone, although some aspects may include family and friends. The most common mistake people make is basing their goals on someone else's. It's a common misconception that everyone wants to earn more money, for example. However, if this wasn't important to you, but you set it as a goal anyway, your actions wouldn't be in alignment, and you'd be less likely to reach your goal. To set goals, you need to be really clear about what you want.

Exercise: Goal-setting

Part A - Goals

I want you to think about your life and where you're at right now. Ask yourself the following question and complete the sentence: Why do you need to set goals for yourself?

I need to set goals for myself because I need …

When creating goals, use **S.M.A.R.T**:

Specific - Be specific about your goal
Measurable - Is your goal realistic?
Achievable - Can you achieve this?
Realistic - Is it realistic?
Timescale - Do you have support?

Set a completion date. Just because you've written down a goal doesn't mean it will magically happen. You need to take action to achieve your goals, and the only way you'll be able to get there is if the goals are reasonable and realistic in the first place. If you set unrealistic goals, you are just setting yourself up for overwhelm, stress and ultimately, failure.

Here are ten questions designed to help you gain clarity on your goal(s):

1.What goal do you want to achieve?

2. What would you like to happen with ______?

3. What do you really want?

4.. What would you like to accomplish?

5.. What result are you trying to achieve?

6.. What outcome would be ideal?

7.. What do you want to change?

8.. Why are you hoping to achieve this goal?

9.. What would the benefits be if you achieved this goal?

Part B – Current Reality

This step helps you gain awareness of your current situation – what's going on, the context and the magnitude of the situation for example.

Take your time to think about the questions and reflect your answers.

Here are 20 questions designed to clarify your current reality:

1. What is happening now (what, who, when, and how often)? What is the effect or result of this?

2. Have you already taken any steps towards your goal?

3. How would you describe what you did?

4. Where are you now in relation to your goal?

5. On a scale of one to ten, where are you?

6. What has contributed to your success so far?

7. What progress have you made so far?

8. What is working well right now?

9. What is required of you?

10. Why haven't you reached that goal already?

11. What do you think is stopping you?

12. What do you think was really happening?

13. Do you know other people who have achieved that goal?

14. What did you learn from _____?

15. What have you already tried?

16. How could you turn this around this time?

17. What could you do better this time?

18. If you asked ____, what would they say about you?

19. On a scale of one to ten how severe/serious/urgent is the situation?

20. If someone said/did that to you, what would you think/feel/do?

Part C - Options

Once you have a clear understanding of your current situation, you are in a better position to consider what to do to reach your goal. Here are 20 questions designed to help you explore options and/or generate solutions:

1. What are your options?

2. What do you think you need to do next?

3. What could be your first step?

4. What do you think you need to do to get a better result (or closer to your goal)?

5. What else could you do?

6. Who else might be able to help?

7. What would happen if you did nothing?

8. What has worked for you already? How could you do more of that?

9. What would happen if you did that?

10. What is the hardest/most challenging part of that for you?

11. What advice would you give to a friend about that?

12. What would you gain/loss by doing/saying that?

13. If someone did/said that to you what do you think would happen?

14. What's the best/worst thing about that option?

15. Which option do you feel ready to act on?

16. How have you tacked this/a similar situation before?

17. What could you do differently?

18. Who do you know who has encountered a similar situation?

19. If anything was possible, what would you do?

20. What else?

Client testimonial: Fear of flying

"From my first contact with Hayley she was great, positive, supportive and had a true 'we can sort this attitude!'. On our first session she made me feel relaxed and at ease and most importantly that I wasn't on my own with my flight anxieties. I had 2x 1.5 sessions with Hayley and in both those sessions talked things through, she gave me some tools to use when things weren't great and also sent me into a deep relaxation (which I have to be honest was amazing!). Afterwards I felt emotionally drained but so relaxed. I am always the biggest sceptic of 'tools' to fix my anxiety but I can genuinely say I followed up on these sessions with the most positive flight I have had in years, I would almost go as far as to say I (nearly) enjoyed it!"
- Leanne Webster

Exercise: 90-Day Plan

Replicate the following worksheets in your journal. Review regularly, track your goals and create a new plan every 90-days.

Goal-setting 90 day plan

BY HAYLEY AUSTIN NLP LIFE COACH

GOALS TO ACHIEVE

Goal 1.

Goal 2.

Goal 3.

WHY I WANT THESE GOALS? - LIST THE BENEFITS HERE

ACHIEVING THESE GOALS WILL HELP ME TO	THE PAIN OF NOT ACHIEVING THESE GOALS IS

Goal-setting 90 day plan

BY HAYLEY AUSTIN NLP LIFE COACH

IN ORDER TO ACHIEVE THIS GOAL I NEED TO BE SOMEBODY THAT WHO? WHAT RESOURCES DO YOU NEED?

Who do I need to become?

What resources do I need?

ACTION STEPS TO TAKE TO ACHIEVE YOUR GOALS

Month 1.

Month 2.

Month 3.

DESCRIBE A DAY IN YOUR LIFE WHEN THIS GOAL HAS BEEN COMLETED?

"Love is the only force capable of transforming an enemy into a friend"

Martin Luther King Jr.

Connection with Self (and the World)

If we could summarise anxiety, it would be the feeling of being unsafe. Yet so many of us feel unsafe by simply being who we are. We are bombarded with messages throughout our lives about who we should be, how we should look, and how we should behave to be accepted by our peers, family and society. Whether we gained these messages from the media, or through parenting and education, we've lived in fear of exposing any parts of us that could be rejected by others. The truth is, many of us don't know who we really are because we've spent so many years adopting masks to hide behind. The fear of revealing our true self and the thought of what people might think is a huge trigger for anxiety.

How we relate to ourselves determines how we relate to the world. The things we judge ourselves for become the things that we judge others for. The ways that we express love depend largely on how we received love throughout childhood, and also the level to which we love ourselves. What we believe influences our actions (or inaction) and prejudices. When we carry shame, it comes out unconsciously at times of stress and conflict, quite often towards our loved ones. When we have low self-esteem, it is expressed through many – often destructive – behaviours, whether it be causing harm to others, the environment, or ourselves.

Disconnection is a significant cause of anxiety. It takes us away from the present, thrusts us into the past or future, and we become consumed by thought. With connection comes presence, and when we can re-connect with self, we create a deeper connection to the people and environment around us.

Exercise: Eye-gazing

Eye-gazing is an incredibly powerful way to connect with others, and especially potent if you feel you have disconnected from a partner. This exercise has the ability to repair a 'broken' relationship! Many of us struggle with intimacy for various reasons, one reason being because we lack connection with ourselves. This can be a very uncomfortable exercise, especially if you're not used to maintaining – or even making - eye-contact. Give it a go. Start slowly and see if you can increase your gaze over time.

Find a partner, sit or stand comfortably, and gaze deep into their eyes, without speaking. You may feel awkward or embarrassed to begin with. Perhaps you'll feel vulnerable and almost 'naked', having someone see you in such a way that you've never felt seen. Feel into your emotions and discomfort as they arise; avoid the temptation to avert your gaze as a way of avoiding the discomfort. Be present, even when it feels uncomfortable. The healing is in the feeling!

What do you see when you gaze into the other person's eyes? What do you feel? In what ways are you seeing them differently? What can you say about your level of connection while you're eye-gazing?

Start by doing this for one minute. Each time you do it with the same partner, increase the time by 30-seconds. Slowly build up to 5-minutes if you're able. If you want to increase intimacy in your relationship, eye-gaze daily!

If you want to improve the relationship you have with yourself, you can also do this on your own by staring in a mirror as part of a self-love exercise. Be warned: it's deeply uncomfortable. We have so much negative self-talk running on repeat daily in our minds that it can be hard to see or accept who we are beyond the chatter. Take it very slowly, one baby step at a time, and show kindness and compassion to yourself, even when the voice inside is screaming at you.

Using meditation to Connect with Self

Life is a story we weave together from the thoughts, feelings, and emotions we experience each moment. Yet we live the majority of our life in the memories of our past and the expectations of the future. Rarely do we live in the present. Past memories and future aspirations that we embrace throughout our lives breed the stresses we feel in each day. In fact, the average person is a bundle of conditioned reflexes and nerves that are constantly triggered by situations and circumstances. There are times in our lives when we feel overwhelmed, pressured and stressed. Meditation is a powerful and effective tool to bring you back to the present moment.

How Does Meditation Work?

We are all engaged in a continuous internal dialogue in which the meaning and emotional associations of one thought trigger the next, usually without our being consciously aware of the process. Buddhist psychology describes this process as samskara, which can be seen as grooves in the mind that make thoughts flow in the same direction. Our personal samskara are created from the memories of our past and can force us to react in the same limited way over and over again. Most people build up their identity based on samskara without even realising they are doing this.

In meditation, we disrupt the unconscious progression of thoughts and emotions by focusing on a new object of attention, whether that is a mantra, our breath, or an image.

Meditation is one of the best ways to loosen the grip of sticky emotions and connect to our true self, which isn't limited, angry, or fearful, but is an infinite source of pure consciousness. Meditation brings us home to the peace of present-moment awareness and gives us an experience of profound relaxation that dissolves fatigue and long-standing stresses and – as countless studies have shown – promotes both physical and emotional healing. The benefits of meditation include:

- lowered blood pressure and hypertension
- slower heart rate
- decreases cholesterol levels
- reduced production of 'stress hormones,' including cortisol and adrenaline

- more efficient oxygen use by the body
- releases feel-good hormones and helps you to connect with yourself on a deeper level.
- improved immune function

Beyond these significant health benefits, the greatest gift of meditation is the sense of calm and inner peace it brings into our daily life. When we meditate, we go beyond the mind's noisy chatter into an entirely different place: the silence of a mind that is not imprisoned by the past or the future.

With regular practice, the expansive awareness you enter during meditation begins to permeate your life outside of your meditation sessions. You might experience flashes of elation and notice feelings of well-being sweeping over you at unexpected moments. You will begin to walk with more buoyancy and feel warmth and peace in your heart. Your thoughts, actions, and reactions are infused with a little more love and mindful attention. All of these are signs that you are living in harmony with your true spiritual self, and the result is a deeper appreciation and a profound awareness of the divine quality of existence.

Meditation needs practice daily, and once you have mastered this, you might choose to incorporate meditation into your daily routine. The best times to meditate are during your power state - first thing in the morning when your state is still in the theta brainwave (first 20 seconds when you wake up) - or last thing at night after you have completed your journaling and are about to go to sleep.

Theta brainwaves occur most often in sleep but are also dominant in deep meditation. Theta is our gateway to learning, memory, and intuition. In theta, our senses are withdrawn from the external world and focused on signals originating from within. We typically experience this twilight state fleetingly as we wake or drift off to sleep. In theta, we are in a dream; vivid imagery, intuition and information beyond our normal conscious awareness. It's where we hold our 'stuff'; our fears, troubled past, and nightmares.

Some people struggle to 'let go' during meditation. Note that you don't need to meditate to enter a meditative state. If meditation doesn't work for you, explore other ways to enter the space within; art, nature and other forms of creativity may allow you to enter a meditative state.

Connect with Your Inner Self Meditation

Meditation written by Hayley Austin for ***personal*** *use only. Not to be recorded, copied or distributed.*

I'd like you to find a comfortable place, somewhere safe and quiet where you will not be disturbed! Sit down, or lay down, whatever feels comfortable. There is no wrong way to meditate.

Take in at least 10 deep breaths: in for 3 through the nose, and out for 5 through the mouth. Inhale and exhale slowly and deeply, until you can feel your body relax.

I want you to visualise a bright light that is shining above you. See the bright, vibrant light shining down on you sending rays of protection to sooth and comfort you.

The rays of energy start at the top of your head and send protection and warmth all the way down to the soles of your feet. Starting at your feet, feel the warmth as it envelopes your feet. You may feel a tingling sensation in your toes. Feel the energy moving up the legs, around the calves and up to your knees. You may feel your legs becoming heavy as they become limp and loose, limp and loose. Feel the energy now moving slowly to your buttocks, around your tummy, and to the small of your back. You are now starting to relax as you feel the warmth comfort you, feeling safe, calm and at ease. The rays of light are now moving up your back toward your shoulders as you feel them drop and relax. The energy now moves onto the top of your head, moving around the eyes, around the ears, nose and mouth. You may feel your tongue relaxing as you leave a little gap between your teeth to allow your tongue to become completely relaxed.

If any part of you does not feel relaxed, move the rays of light - full of warming energy - to the muscle, and let it envelop you, to soothe and comfort you. Relaxing all your muscles, nerves and fibres in your body.

Feeling safe, calm and secure.

Now take yourself to a place where you feel safe. This could be a beach, a waterfall, or a beautiful forest. Anywhere you feel safe and secure. Take yourself there now. Feel what you can feel, all the happy feelings. See everything around you. Notice what is on the floor; any particular objects. Hear what you can hear; any familiar sounds and smells. Get deep inside your subconscious mind and go to your favourite place.

Now turn your attention inward...even more deeply inside...to find your true authentic self.

Begin by reflecting upon your values. What is most important to you in life? What do you value? Where does your sense of right and wrong come from? Spend the next few moments thinking about your values.

The values you have been thinking form part of the core of who you are. If you are being true to your values, these core beliefs will drive your behaviour.

It feels good to behave in ways that are consistent with your values. For example, if honesty is something you value, this could be reflected in your life by being truthful. If you value your family, perhaps your life reflects this in the time you spend with family members.

Think about how your values could be a part of your day-to-day life.

Now consider what else makes you who you are. Finding your authentic self involves learning who you are. Your authentic self is the real you, the person you are truly meant to be. Your authentic self is the person you are at the core, the person you can be if nothing holds you back.

Imagine the person you believe yourself to be right now. It's okay if you aren't quite sure who you are - just picture yourself going about the things you usually do in a typical day. Imagine that you are watching yourself, observing yourself going about your usual activities.

Picture this person before you and imagine all the things that get in the way of success - circumstances, lack of resources, lack of forgiveness, illness, baggage from the past, anything that is holding this person back in any way at all.

See these problems dissolving...disappearing...going away.

Now imagine this person, standing in the empty room. What is left? Who is this person when all those barriers are stripped away?

Who is this person now? Think about your personality, how you feel. Become at peace with yourself and embrace the real, authentic, genuine you.

Imagine something that makes you feel happy. What is it?

Think of some things you enjoy, things that you like to do.

Now picture yourself as a child. See the world through your younger self's eyes.

What did you want to be when you grew up? What hopes did you have for your future self? What dreams did you have as a child?

What do these aspirations say about who you are?

I want you to visualise a mirror and see yourself achieving your goals and dreams and behaving in a way that makes you feel happy. Picture you doing your daily activities with all the confidence you desire. See yourself being and acting in a way that makes you feel happy and confident. Now step into this image and feel all the glory, happiness and confidence. Notice how you stand tall as you embrace your true self. See what you can see. Get inside the feeling.

Now imagine yourself waking up in the morning as your happy self, practising gratitude and now say these words to you and repeat.

I am loved and love others.

I am honest and true to myself.

I respect myself and treat others with respect.

I am happy.

I can achieve my goals and dreams.

I am ready to take action.

I am my true authentic self.

Now it's time to come back into the room. I'd like you to slowly let the images you have created fade away into the distance and become aware of the sounds you can hear in the room and around you and 1 2 3 open your eyes and come back to the present time. Feeling refreshed, calm and confident in every way.

Improving Self-Esteem and Confidence

A lack of self-esteem or self-confidence can have a knock-on effect across all areas of our lives, from relationships and work to mental health. Low self-esteem or confidence can cripple us, leading to anxiety and an inability to express our true self. There is a difference between the two: self-confidence is faith in your abilities, whereas self-esteem is faith in yourself. For example, you may have the ability to sing in a room full of people, but not believe you're any good at it. However, these aren't so much personality traits as skills that can be practised and improved upon. It can be hard work, but if you are patient with yourself, there are numerous ways you can boost your confidence and self-esteem.

Self-esteem

Self-esteem is more than just self-confidence. The very word itself tells us why it's important; it comes from a Latin word 'aestimare' - to put a value on. Self-esteem is literally the value we place on ourselves. Many of us would have been told - implicitly or explicitly - that we were not good enough as children. Over time, the negative messages we received would have chipped away at our self-esteem until we entered adulthood and lost all belief and confidence in ourselves.

If you have low self-esteem, you may struggle to generalise from the good results you are getting. You may feel uncomfortable hearing and receiving praise, not believing it to be true. You may underachieve and fall short of your potential, or never feel good enough despite your accomplishments. You may spend a whole lifetime underestimating yourself and feeling unworthy.

People with high self-esteem have a strong sense of self: they like themselves, they can recognise and manage their internal state, and they have a clear purpose. The good news is, 'What others can do, you can learn.'

Exercise: Self-Esteem Evaluation

To evaluate your level of self-esteem, take a moment to reflect on the following questions. You may want to meditate and then write down the answers in your journal.

Can I take a compliment without deflecting it, or without qualifying it in my head?

Can I list 5 things I like about myself without hesitating?

How do I react to trying new things?

What am I telling myself when I'm about to do something challenging?

Reflect on the answers: do they suggest that you like yourself?

Here are some simple ways to boost your self-esteem. If you practise them daily, you will notice the way you feel about yourself start to shift positively.

Take a compliment

When you have low self-esteem, accepting a compliment can be a challenge. We question the other person's motives or automatically disbelieve them. Or we deflect attention away from us altogether, deeming ourselves not worthy enough, and quickly pay a compliment to the other person in return. The simplest and most effective way to take a compliment is to say, 'thank you.' Practice in front of a mirror. Hear the compliment in your head or say it out loud and say, 'thank you,' with a smile.

Learn to like yourself

List everything you can think of that you like about yourself. Do this over a week. Look at your values, beliefs, your environment, and your behaviour. Think about the qualities that make you you. Think about a close friend or family member and make a mental note of everything that you love about them. Notice how easy it is to focus on the positives of someone else? Now see yourself through the same eyes of love, kindness and compassion. You may be surprised how long your list becomes.

Try new things

If you suffer from anxiety and fear, spell out the worst-case scenario in your mind. Sometimes this is enough to make you realise how unlikely the fear really is. Think about someone who likes trying new things and the way they would go about trying something new.

Voice your fears

Fear and lack of belief in yourself can stop you from moving forward. When you keep your worries locked away in your mind, they have a hold over you and drive your behaviour. Voicing them allows you to integrate your whole brain - language and logic engaging to calm the amygdala - so that your fears lose their grip. Ask a friend to sit and listen as you run through a fear inventory. They don't need to speak, simply act as a sounding board for your voice to be heard. You may find that as you start talking, more fears that you had no conscious awareness of arise. The talking process enables you to access your inner wisdom and gain clarity. If no one is around, speak to a wall (literally) - it has the same effect.

People with self-esteem don't need to prove themselves. They don't boast, put others down, show off, name drop, dominate the conversation or centre themselves. High self-esteem looks like this: quietly confident, accepting of compliments (without fishing for them), humble, interested in others, and not in need of external validation or recognition.

Exercise: Daily Journaling

Ask yourself:

How do I feel today?

What is important to me today?

What can I do for myself today?

How do I know I have achieved something today?

As the day goes on be mindful of these questions. When you find yourself focusing on the negative and all that has gone wrong in the day, shift your focus to the positives.

Exercise: Qualities and Achievements

Take a piece of paper and draw a line down the middle. On one side write down your good qualities and, on the other, your achievements. These could be as simple as, 'I make people smile,' or 'I taught myself how to cook.' Go back as far in time as you can and reflect on every small accomplishment.

Try to fill the page. This can feel hard but remember that it's OK to recognise positive aspects about yourself. Instead of focusing on your mistakes, draw positives from your experiences. For example, you may think about a past relationship and the things that went wrong. What if you could focus on the good memories? What if you could see the valuable lessons you learned during that relationship or its end as being a positive learning experience in your life? Remind yourself that no-one is perfect, and we can learn from things that go wrong. In fact, our greatest lessons arise from our greatest struggles; every challenge is an opportunity to learn and grow.

Fake It 'Til You Make It!

You may have heard the expression 'fake it 'til you make it!' In NLP terms we call this modelling ourselves and works on the basis that if we embody who we want to be, that's who we eventually become. Sometimes putting on a display of confidence, even if you don't feel it, can change how others perceive and interact with you, and give you a boost. Try the following, which can give the impression of confidence:

Walk tall – stand up straight and look ahead when you walk.

Speak slowly – less confident people tend to rush when they talk.

Wear brighter colours and clothes that make you feel good.

Don't cross your arms – this posture that displays defensiveness or nervousness. Instead, adopt a more open posture by keeping your arms at your sides or on your hips.

Make eye contact when you talk – you can practice this by meeting someone's eyes for three seconds, then looking away for one.

Avoid putting yourself down in conversations (but keep the ability to laugh at yourself).

Visualise someone you know that is confident and mirror their mannerisms.

Confidence

'Low self-confidence isn't a life sentence. Self-confidence can be learned, practised, and mastered--just like any other skill. Once you master it, everything in your life will change for the better.' - Barrie Davenport

Self-confident people inspire confidence in others. They face their fears head-on and tend to be risk takers. They know that no matter what obstacles come their way, they can get past them. Self-confident people tend to see their lives in a positive light even when things aren't going so well, and they are typically satisfied with and respect themselves.

Wouldn't it be amazing to have this kind of self-confidence, every day of the week? I'll let you into a secret – you can!

When we are brimming with self-confidence, we are focused, motivated and feeling 'right' about things. That sense of certainty radiates and attracts others who respond to us positively. We energetically attract good vibes because we are creating them. We draw success into our lives. When we do not feel confident success can feel out of our reach.

The word confidence means different things to different people; it's a personal quality. What does confidence mean to you?

Exercise: What Does Confidence Mean to You?

Complete the following statements. Your answers will help you to determine where you need to make changes in your life. Be as open and honest as you can without attaching any judgement to your answers.

1. When I am feeling confident I am..............................

2. Self-doubt makes me.................................

3. My self-worth is high when...........................

4. I know that I am right when.........................

5. I am at my best in relationships when........................

6. I lose confidence in myself when...........................

7. When I am facing a big challenge I....................

8. If someone criticises me, I feel.....................

Whatever confidence means to us, we can all agree on this: it feels good. So how can we get more of this feel-good factor?

Step 1: Decide to Change. Get clear about what you want and why. You need to be ready and willing to step up and make the necessary changes to be the best version of you. You are saying, 'Here I am and, I am going to take control.' Say it! Feels good right? You are in charge; believe this!

Step 2: Know Your Worth. You need to know your true worth and value. You will face many challenges, but with a positive approach, you can find the inner strength you need. Learn what it takes to be a success and stay cool and calm so that you can deal with whatever life throws at you.

Step 3: Believe in Yourself. All that is truly holding you back is you and your lack of self-belief. When self-doubt creeps in, focus on your future self and make the changes needed. Focus on what you can do, not what you can't.

Step 4: Get Going! If you have passion, you can do what you want. With a can-do approach, anything is possible. Goal set and plan. Go-getters are not people pleasers; they know what they want and follow through. The time is now. Stop procrastinating - take action!

Step 5: Love Your Life. This is the link between happiness and confidence. Life is like a rollercoaster; your ability to ride the up's and downs will determine your level of success and fulfilment. Love and appreciate each part of your life - even through challenging times - for a more positive outcome.

Step 6: Be a Winner. Be the very best you can be and help others to rise. When you know you have given it your best shot, no matter what happens, you will feel a sense of self-respect. A life well lived is a fast-track route to confidence and strong self-belief. When you are confident, you attract the very best of what life has to offer.

Step 7: Take Positive Action. How do we create our own reality? By taking responsibility for ourselves and stop being a victim. We can get caught up in a victim mindset, believing that life is happening to us and there's nothing we can do to change our circumstances. When we take responsibility, we're far more likely to take positive action. Taking charge of your life - instead of dwelling on all that is wrong with it - will give you a massive boost and help your motivation and energy. This one thing can change the trajectory of your life!

Exercise: Boosting Your Confidence with Anchoring (NLP)

Think of a specific time when you felt confident (not excited, nervous or unsure). It can be as simple as a time you went to the shops to get some milk, or anything else you are used to and comfortable doing.

Now vividly imagine being in your body again during that memory. Notice what you feel, what you see and what you hear. Mostly notice any feelings in your body as these are the most important. Notice your posture when you are comfortable doing something.

Now as you are vividly imagining the specific event just press your fingertip of one hand onto a knuckle of your other hand. Hold it for 10 to 15 seconds as you allow the feeling of confidence to peak. And then release. The idea here is to anchor in the feeling of confidence.

Repeat that process with a minimum of three confident experiences you can think of. Be sure to use the same knuckle. Next time you feel nervous in a situation, go ahead and press that knuckle and hold it for 10-15 seconds. Notice how your nervousness disappears as you activate the anchored state of comfortable confidence. Be sure to regularly recharge the anchor because every use weakens it.

Busting Limiting Beliefs

Your limiting decisions have shaped everything you do and have impacted how you show up in the world. They have prevented you from seeing opportunities and maybe even discouraged you from trying at all. Your true self may have a deep desire to express herself on stage, but your belief that you're not good enough may have led you to suppress that part of yourself. We all have beliefs that limit us, sometimes buried so deep we're not consciously aware of them.

What are limiting beliefs?

Limiting beliefs are those which constrain us in some way. Just by believing them, we do not think, do or say the things that they inhibit. And in doing so, we impoverish our lives.

We may have beliefs about rights, duties, abilities, permissions and so on. Limiting beliefs are often about ourselves and our self-identity. The beliefs may also be about other people and the world in general. In any case, they sadly limit us. To identify your limiting beliefs, start by considering what you say and the language you use around specific things. For example, if you're having trouble finding a relationship, what are the reasons you give? Perhaps you say, 'Women only want men who have a lot of money,' or 'Guys are only interested in younger women.' Anything you say to yourself to justify why something isn't working out for you is a limiting belief.

Your belief will sound perfectly reasonable, valid and true to you, and your brain will seek lots of evidence to support it. Perhaps it's been your experience and a pattern to date, so you've adopted it as truth. Regardless, limiting beliefs get in the way of what you want and who you want to be.

I do/don't

We may define ourselves by what we do or do not do. I may say, 'I am an accountant,' which means I do not do marketing and should not even think about it, and consequently fail to sell my services well. Another common limiting belief is around how we judge ourselves. We think 'I don't deserve...' and so do not expect or seek things.

I can't

We often have limited self-images of what we can and cannot do. If I think 'I cannot sing,' then I will never try or not go to singing lessons to improve my ability. This is the crux of many 'I can't' statements: we believe our abilities are fixed and that we cannot learn.

I must/mustn't

We are bound by values, norms, laws and other rules that constrain what we must and must not do. However, not all of these are mandatory, and some are distinctly limiting. If I think 'I must clean the house every day,' then this robs me of time that may be spent doing something more productive.

I am/am not

The verb 'to be' is quite a pernicious little thing and as we think 'I am,' we also think 'I am not,' or 'I cannot'. For example, we may think 'I am an artist,' and so conclude that we can never be any good at mathematics, or must not soil our hands with manual work.

'I am' thinking assumes we cannot change. Whether I think 'I am intelligent,' or 'I am not intelligent', either belief may stop me from seeking to learn. 'I am' also leads to generalisation, for example, where 'I am stupid' becomes 'all of me is all of stupid and all of stupid is all of me.' A better framing is to connect the verb to the individual act, such as, 'That was a stupid thing to do.'

When coupled with values we get beliefs about whether a person is right or wrong, good or bad.

Others are/will

Just as we have limiting beliefs about ourselves, we also have beliefs about other people, which can limit us in many ways. If we think others are more capable and superior, then we will not challenge them. If we see them as selfish, we may not ask them for help.

We often guess what others are thinking based on our 'theory of mind' and beliefs about them. These guesses are often wrong. Hence, we may believe they do not like us when they actually have no particular opinion and think we are rather nice. When we guess their thoughts, we then deduce their likely actions, which can, of course, be completely wrong. Faced with this evidence, it is surprising how many will still hold to the original beliefs.

How the world works

Beyond the limiting beliefs above there can be all kinds of belief about 'how the world works,' from laws of nature to the property of materials. This can lead to anything from the beliefs that all dogs will bite, to the idea that aeroplane travel is dangerous.

Why do we limit our beliefs?

Experience

A key way by which we form our beliefs is through our direct experiences. We act, something happens, and we draw conclusions. Often such beliefs are helpful, but they can also be very limiting. Particularly when we are young and have few experiences, we may form false and limiting conclusions. Nature builds us this way to keep us out of harm's way. We learn and build beliefs faster from harmful experiences. Sticking my finger on a hot stove hurts a lot so we believe all stoves are dangerous and never touch a stove again.

Education

When forming our perceptions of the world, we cannot depend on experiences for everything. We hence read and listen to parents and teachers about how the world works and how to behave in it. But our teachers are not always well informed, they themselves operating from their own belief systems which in turn come with limitations. We also learn from what peers tell us and are influenced - and 'infected' - by their beliefs, which may be very limiting.

Education is a double-edged sword as it tells you what is right or wrong, good or bad. It helps you survive and grow, but just because you were told something, you may never try new things and so miss pleasant and useful experiences and knowledge.

Faulty logic

In decisions, we make 'return on investment' estimations and easily conclude that the investment of time, effort and money is insufficient and that there is a low chance of success and a high chance of failure. The return may even be negative as we are harmed in some way.

People make many decision errors, for example, based on poor estimation of probabilities. We take a little data and generalise it to everything. We go on hunches that are based more on subconscious hopes and fears than on reality.

The word 'because' can be surprisingly hazardous. When we use it, it seems like we are using good reason, but this may not be so. We like to understand cause-and-effect and often do not challenge reasoning that uses the mechanisms of rational argument.

Excuse

One reason we use faulty logic and form limiting beliefs is to excuse ourselves from what we perceive to be our failures. When we do something and it does not work, we often explain away our failure by forming and using beliefs which justify our actions and leave us blameless. But in doing so, we do not learn and may increasingly paint ourselves into a corner, limiting what we will think and do in the future.

Fear

Limiting beliefs are often fear-driven. Locking the belief in place is the fear that, if we go against the beliefs, deep needs will be harmed. There is often a strong social component to our decisions and the thought of criticism, ridicule or rejection by others is enough to powerfully inhibit us. We also fear that we may be harmed in some way by others, and so avoid them or seek to appease them.

Here's how you can change self-limiting beliefs using NLP techniques:

1. Get into the habit of modifying any negative statement about yourself from present to past. Statements made in the present tense trick the body into believing this statement to be a current reality. Statements made in the past imply that the event has come and gone, creating a transition that opens up new, future possibilities. So, for example, instead of saying, 'I am so disorganised,' modify this by saying, 'I have been so disorganised in the past, but I'm so much more on top of things now.' Even if you don't feel comfortable modifying the statement, just replacing 'am' with 'have been' will create a shift in your reality

2. Identify a specific outcome you want to achieve. Pick the date in the future you want this outcome to occur by. Utilising the power of future mental imagery, imagine that this desired outcome has already happened, referencing that future date as having already occurred, e.g. it's August 31, 2020, and I have spoken on stage in front of 5,000 people.

Make this a daily practice. Every day, or as often as possible, spend some time immersing yourself in this mental imagery. Imagine the details of the future event as if it happened in the past in full technicolour. How does your body feel? What are your emotions like? How did people around you react when the event occurred? I suggest dedicating at least 15 minutes to this visualization practice to make it feel real.

3. Focus on a specific area of your life – finances, relationships, work or health – and write a list of beliefs you have around it. You may want to spend 10-minutes meditating beforehand to access your unconscious mind and enter a state of free-flow writing. Review the list objectively and, with your hand on your heart, ask yourself if each belief is true. Drop into your heart space and notice how the belief feels; you will fill a deep knowing and sense of calm if something is untrue. Notice when your ego wants to jump in and talk you into believing something to be true. If it helps, imagine that one of your friends is standing in front of and sharing a limiting belief. I'm sure you'd find plenty of examples of why their belief isn't true. Extend the same kindness and compassion to yourself as you go through this exercise.

Exercise: How to Expand Your Comfort Zone

This exercise is going to help you expand your comfort zone, by exploring where the boundaries currently sit. You will identify what you would like to have within an expanded comfort zone.

1. Get a large piece of paper and some coloured pens. Stick a photo of you right in the middle of the paper. Think about

everything you feel safe and confident doing. Write these thoughts down on the paper next to your photograph. The more relaxed you feel about these thoughts the closer they should be to your photograph. You can focus on as much content as you like.

2. Now take a different coloured pen and draw a rough circle which encloses all the things you have just written down about yourself. This is your comfort zone! There was a time where everything in this circle was unknown, but you learned to do everything you can see here. You learned, modelled and challenged yourself; now these things that you do are easy and comfortable with you.

3. After you have completed your comfort map, please move onto the next stage. I want you to write a list of things that you would like to do - one you want to do not what would please others! Put in the things you want but currently not doing. Now write this list inside the map, outside of your comfort zone circle, again putting the things easier closer to you and other things that are harder away from you.

4. For now, take a look at the thing that is nearest the outside edge of your comfort zone – maybe even sitting on the boundary. Have a think about what it would look like when you have done that. How pleased you will be with yourself. What is the first step you need to take to get there? Repeat this for the second and third etc…

5. Take a deep breath and start working towards that one thing. Remember, it's nearly in your comfort zone already, so all you need to do is expand your boundary. Once you feel ready, start picking

off things one at a time, until one day in the not too distant future, you will realise that everything currently in your possibility zone has moved into your expanded zone, and your possibility zone is full of new possibilities.

You might be feeling anxious and fear may set in whilst you do this activity. The what if questions may appear. My advice to you is to feel the fear and DO IT ANYWAY. Action is what it takes to become a master at what you are trying to achieve.

Exercise: Being at Cause

Make a list of all the excuses you have for not changing something.

Review your list. How many of the things that you have written down can you get around if you really wanted to? How many of these things can you ignore? How many of these things would change if you just got going?

Ask yourself...

What are you not doing that you could be doing?

What is stopping you?

For most people, it is limiting beliefs holding them back. For me, these little monsters are like little bundles of energy in red suits with little chains that they wrap around me and pull me back. I have a very strong visual imagination, I know! These little monsters tell me that it's too scary, it won't work, it's too difficult, or no-one will like what I am doing - a mass of wasted energy called self-doubt or self-sabotage.

What do your feelings of self-doubt look like? Identify these if you can. Take 5-minutes and think about all the times you self-sabotaged your efforts and how this made you feel. What can you see and hear? Write these feelings down. If it helps, use colour to represent your feelings of self-doubt. Mine is red!

Your Unconscious Mind

Do you have an attic or a cellar in your house? Or a room that you have used to store stuff in for years? Over time this space becomes cluttered and untidy. You could have old pictures, baby clothes, old toys, old collections, and all sorts of other 'stuff' you've been hoarding. There may be something useful in there, but you'd struggle to find it.

Much of our past is stored in our unconscious mind - a bit like that attic or cellar! Our mind is full of things that may be helpful if only we could find them, but also full of stuff that is taking up space and holding us back.

Your unconscious mind is amazing. It is where every memory, experience, belief, value and learning is stored. You have a lot of useful information stored in your unconscious (subconscious) mind. For example, could you imagine having to consciously think about how to drive each day? Thanks to our unconscious mind, we can drive pretty much on autopilot!

Science shows that most of our decisions, actions, emotions and behaviour depend on the 95% of brain activity that is beyond our conscious awareness, which means that 95 – 99% of our life comes from the programming in our subconscious mind. Without your subconscious mind, you cannot recall your childhood experiences, past lives etc. The use of positive affirmations helps the subconscious mind to reprogram through repeated personal, positive, present tense statements that can override the negative belief or negative thoughts already registered.

Now I want you to think of a memory. Have you ever experienced a smell of something – a certain perfume, aftershave or flower, even a cooking smell – and being transported to the past? Sometimes this can happen to you, and you had not thought about that memory in years. This is because we have (what we call in NLP terms) anchored the memory with a smell.

Exercise: Tidying up the Unconscious Mind

1. Find a quiet place where you will not be disturbed. Tell yourself that you are going to do some visualisation. You will need to close your eyes for this task. Everyone can visualise. Visualise your front door - what colour is it? Ok, so now you understand what visualising is (and how easy it is), let's continue.

2. Imagine you are sat on a really comfortable chair, watching a screen in front of you. Let an image of a large attic appear on the screen.

3. Ask your unconscious mind to associate the items in the attic with parts of you: your fears, your dreams, your beliefs, past problems, current challenges. Some things that you no longer need to carry around!

4. Ask your unconscious mind to begin tidying the attic and reorganise it in a way that works for you. Allow yourself to be drawn to things that can be thrown away, what you need to keep for now, and other stuff that you need to ignore.

5. Be relaxed and accept that you don't need to know why or how - your unconscious mind will simply do this for you. Ask it! You needed this stuff once, it did serve a purpose, but now you no longer need it you can let it go. , Ask your unconscious mind to organise the attic - full of the things that are still useful to you and you want to keep - to make it easily accessible.

6. You can now return to the attic as many times as you like to reorganise things. And while your unconscious mind continues all by itself, you can open your eyes and come back into the room.

Trying to achieve a goal with a limiting belief is like climbing a mountain while carrying a 100-lb pack. You may begin enthusiastically, but soon each step will feel hard and painful, and your progress will slow to a crawl. Instead of pushing yourself to climb harder, a better choice would be to lighten your pack by dumping the limiting belief that's holding you back. Some people, however, become so attached to that 100-lb pack that they won't let it go no matter how restricting it is. Instead, they blame the mountain, the rocks, or their shoes for their troubles. But for highly conscious, growth-seeking people, eventually there comes a time to release the old baggage. The lighter pack may feel strange at first, but it will soon enable more rapid progress, and the climb will be more enjoyable as well.

Changing your beliefs can be unsettling at first. But like all change, you get used to it. And once you do it enough times, you may even come to enjoy the process.

Exercise: Do You Really Believe That?

1. I would like you to take your journal or a pad of paper and write 2 lists. one list is for the limiting beliefs you currently have about yourself, the other is for the great, empowering beliefs that you have. Most people find it easy to come up with four or five items on each list. As you write, keep asking yourself, 'And what else?' Keep going until you have at least 10 items in each list.

2. Look at your list carefully and identify the three beliefs in each list that have the most impact on your life - three great beliefs that you would not want to let go of and three limiting beliefs that are holding you back in a big way.

3. Identify how you can maximise or power up the impact of the great beliefs.

4. Now look at your limiting beliefs – the three biggies that are seriously holding you back. Visually imagine carrying them around with you all the time every day. Like a stack of heavy

weights that you are carrying around. As you go through life, imagine these beliefs as weights getting heavier and heavier as you continue to live in the future. Horrible feeling, right?

5. Are you ready to change? Take 2 of these beliefs and write down what immediate change you can make and what you would like to believe instead.

6. Now challenge yourself to find evidence of the limiting beliefs not being true. This process loosens the old belief. At the same time, you start to build a strong scaffold that will take you towards your new belief.

7. From now on focus on these new sets of beliefs. Repeat these new beliefs every day as you wake up and say them again before bedtime.

Now we have completed a few exercises and identified limiting beliefs, I will show you how to install new beliefs into your storage system aka memory. Enjoy seeing the world from a new perspective.

Exercise: Creating New Beliefs and Storing Them in Your Subconscious

1. Think of a belief you have that you no longer want.

2. Float up above your memory storage system, so that you have a bird's eye view.

3. Float all the way back through your memory storage system until you find the point at which you developed that limiting belief.

4. Ask yourself what you can learn from the event - this is important; take time to think about this one.

5. Go back in just before the event happened and transmit additional resources - both to yourself and anyone else involved in the incident - that would have enabled you to develop a different and more empowering belief.

6. In your own time float all the way back to the present, noticing how different everything is for you, living your life with a different belief, and with the new learning.

7. Feel confident about going forwards in the future.

This process works by immersing yourself in the new belief until your subconscious accepts it as true and integrates it into your mental operating system. My favourite method is to use visualisation, but some people swear by verbal affirmations, especially when combined with strong emotion.

Be patient with yourself because it can take a while for new beliefs to take hold. It usually takes me anywhere from a few weeks to several months before I've successfully integrated a new belief into my subconscious, depending on my internal resistance. If there's no resistance, I can install a new belief in a day, but that's rare for significant changes. It takes time for my mind to accept the new belief as fact instead of merely considering it as a possibility or an interesting idea, and it has to be successfully integrated with all the other thoughts going through my head. Installing a new belief is like getting an organ transplant. It takes a while for your body to accept the new organ, and there's always a risk of rejection.

You'll know when your new belief has taken root because you'll begin to act in accordance with it without even thinking about it consciously. It will feel just like any other belief to you, no different from a belief in gravity. The key to success when forming new beliefs is to practice them every day.

Exercise: Busting Your Limiting Beliefs

Identify a belief that is holding you back, and then work through the questions to discover the truth or falsity of your fearful thoughts. Use the process to tap into the limiting belief, and ultimately let it go. I recommend working through this exercise slowly, taking pauses as needed. You might like to close your eyes to go deeper. Just relax and observe what comes up.

What is the belief you wish to work on? (For example, I'm not good enough, my partner doesn't care about me, my family doesn't approve).

Is it true? Is it really true? Can you absolutely know for sure it is true, or do you just believe it to be true based on past experiences?

Is it true? Is it really true?

What is the payoff? What are the benefits of you holding on to this belief? How does it serve you?

What is the cost? How does it alter who you are? How does it affect your behaviours? How does it impact on your attitudes?

How do you feel? What emotions arise? What behaviours or addictions does it evoke? How do you treat yourself and others when you think about it?

How do you react when you think about this limiting belief, fear, thought?

What images come to mind when you believe this thought?

What other fears does it spark?

Does this thought bring peace or stress into your life?

Can you see a stress-free reason to hold onto the belief?

Can you see a reason to drop this belief?

Who would you be without this thought?

Now turn the belief into a positive. If your belief was, 'I can never make enough money,' then the new thought becomes, 'I can always make enough money.'

Is your new thought as true or more true than the original belief?

If you lived this new thought, what would you do differently?

"I am enough"

Brené Brown

Children and Anxiety

Anxiety in children is on the increase with children being affected by younger and younger ages. Childhood anxiety manifests quite differently to that in adults, and we often misread the signs and instead label an anxious child as being 'difficult', 'defiant' or 'too sensitive'. The purpose of this chapter is to help you spot the signs and support your child through their anxiety so that as they develop and grow, they have accessible tools to manage their anxiety through to adulthood.

We are born with only two fears: the fear of falling, and the fear of noise. Everything else is learned through our environment, experience and the modelling of the people around us. Indeed, a fear of spiders can be learned from a parent who fears spiders. My son developed a fear of spiders after witnessing me freak out about one. He associated my reaction (which scared him) with the spider; my reaction was imprinted into his psyche more so than the spider itself.

Many anxieties and fears start when we are young. Typically, we experience something that creates fear which becomes stored as a memory in our unconscious mind. How we remember a memory will be via our five senses. We may have seen or heard something that triggered a fear response or felt pain and hurt. Fears feel greater when we have been unable to process them fully. Maybe we needed to cry - a powerful emotional release - but were told not to, so stuffed the emotion down. Perhaps we needed to talk to someone but didn't know how, so suppressed our thoughts and feelings. The event could have been something as innocuous as a dog unexpectedly jumping up at a toddler, creating a fear of dogs. As children grow and develop, a sound, smell or sight of something specific can reawaken the unconscious memory, trigger an emotional response and lead to all kinds of behaviours.

Unlike adults with our fully developed brain, children have less ability to control their behaviour, especially in times of reactivity. When they're in the stress response, their brain shuts down; it's not the time for logic or reasoning. Unfortunately, many of us can become reactive to our children, meeting their stress with our own, causing their feelings of disorientation and fear to escalate. If we are to support our children through their anxiety, we first need to address our own.

Anxiety is an intense feeling of fear or worry and can cause a problem if a child feels unable to gain control of these emotions. Children need to feel safe, and anxiety can leave them feeling very unsafe, insecure and, consequently, out of control. When a child experiences unwanted physiological symptoms that contribute to feeling out of control and off balance, they can become reactive, either physically, emotionally or behaviourally. Anxiety is often difficult for children and young people to describe, so symptoms are typically identified from the young person's behaviour. Separation anxiety, restlessness, sleep issues, panic attacks, skin picking, and stomach problems can all be ascribed to feelings of anxiety.

Signs of Anxiety in Children

Physical Signs of Anxiety

- Frequently complains of headaches or stomach aches
- Refuses to eat snacks or lunch at day-care or school
- Will avoid using the toilet except at home
- Has difficulty falling asleep
- Easily distracted, restless, fidgety, or hyperactive
- Constantly tenses his muscles

Emotional Signs of Anxiety

- Cries frequently
- Has meltdowns and tantrums that may not seem age appropriate
- Acts extremely sensitive
- Is afraid of making mistakes
- Is scared of getting into trouble (and feels a lot of shame when they do)
- Becomes moody or angry for no apparent reason.
- Has panic attacks (or is afraid of having panic attacks).
- Has phobias (about bees, dogs, etc.) and exaggerated fears (about things like natural disasters, etc.).
- Worries about things that are far in the future

- Can be clingy in social situations
- Is worried or afraid during drop-offs (at school, relatives' homes etc.)
- Gets distracted from playing by their worries and fears.
- Has obsessive thoughts or compulsive behaviours (finger tapping, hand washing, etc.).
- Perfectionism, fearing making mistakes and having a strong emotional reaction when they do

Behavioural Signs of Anxiety

- Asks 'what if?' constantly.
- Avoids participating during circle time or other class activities.
- Avoids things they find hard
- Refuses to go to school
- A need to control the behaviour of others, particularly in play
- A strong need to be 'good' for fear of repercussions
- Avoids social situations with peers after school or on weekends (extracurricular activities, birthday parties, etc.).
- Refuses to speak to peers or strangers in stores, restaurants, etc.
- Becomes emotional or angry when separating from parents or loved ones.
- Constantly seeks approval from parents, teachers and friends.
- Says 'I can't do it!' without a real reason.

Anxiety and fear are just as valid and important as any other human emotion; they serve to protect us. In the absence of fear, I dare say the human race would have become extinct a long time ago! Our flight-or-flight response exists to alert us to potential danger so that we can act quickly and helps us to gain trust in ourselves and our instincts and to guide us as we take risks. Accepting there is a part of us that is scared of something is good. It's essential for adults to model that we too feel scared at times, to show our children that it's perfectly natural and normal.

Anxiety has three different components, starting with anxious thoughts. 'What if they don't like me?', 'Will I embarrass myself?', 'Is there a monster under the bed?', 'Will I get it wrong?' are just some of the thoughts our children experience. As adults - perceiving the world through an adult lens that, even if we ourselves are experiencing anxiety, can rationalise our experiences using our maturely developed brain - we typically try to 'fix' our children, downplaying their worries or telling them that it will be okay. We want to protect them from the world; no one wants to see their child struggling or unhappy. Sometimes when we recognise their triggers, we may want to avoid stressful situations altogether. We have the best of intentions, but often this leads to children avoiding rather than fully processing and integrating their experiences which can increase anxiety later on. We'll cover more effective ways to support your child later!

Once the anxious thoughts creep in, a physical reaction happens. The adrenalin (fight-or-flight) kicks in as the body prepares to protect itself. Hands become sweaty, the heart quickens, children feel butterflies in their stomach, or they develop tummy aches and feel sick. These are genuine reactions caused by the adrenalin. Their body is ready to flee or fight. These sensations can feel particularly hard for young children. Big emotions are uncomfortable and scary for small children, who are still learning how to self-regulate.

Understandably, once your child has experienced all of this, it affects how they behave. They could go quiet, or they could have a tantrum. They could get clingy or lash out. They could struggle to sleep or be tired all the time. As each child is unique, how they react when anxious will be different to the next child.

How to Support Your Child

Manage your own anxiety

One of the first things you can do to support your child is by managing your own anxiety. Luckily, you have this book to assist you. Quite often, when we are in an anxious state and starting to feel overwhelmed, we too enter our fight-or-flight mode and become reactive, projecting our stress onto our children - even if just energetically - exacerbating theirs. Take a couple of tools from this book to have at your disposal in those times when you can feel your anxiety bubbling to the surface and introduce more self-care - however that looks for you - to give you space to breathe and recharge. For some simple wellness tips, turn back to page 36.

Validate their experience

'I know you're scared, and that's okay, and I'm here, and I'm going to help you get through this.'

It's paramount that we validate our child's experience. Everyone wants to feel seen and heard, and ultimately our children want to feel loved, safe and have a sense of belonging. Anxiety can hit at the most 'inconvenient' of moments - as you're rushing out the door, or when you're about to jump on an important call - and as a parent, it's so easy to get consumed by our own frustrations and experience of our child's behaviour at that moment. Pause to breathe before responding and connect with your child. When a child feels anxious, they need to feel safe. They need to know that it is safe to express their emotions without shame or judgment. The calmer you are, the easier it is for them to calm their nervous system and work through their anxiety.

Talk about it when things have calmed down

Trying to talk to and reason with a child amidst a stressful or anxious episode is like trying to drive without any gas; it won't work. The upper part of a child's brain - the thinking brain - is cut off; they can't think clearly or even fully listen. The more you talk about something in the moment that it's happening, the more it will feed the anxiety. Anxiety does, after all, feed on fear! When our children feel anxious, they need to make their world right. Their brain will seek evidence to support their reactions. Lots of discussion at the time will only prove that it is a 'big thing' and they will start to create an identity around it. Deal with it - and any 'unwanted' behaviours - later, when things have calmed down, and your child is able to engage their whole brain and actively listen. Talk about what they could do 'next time' they start to feel a certain way. Come up with a game plan. It won't necessarily be followed but if you can provide your child with their own tools that they can access when needed, over time - as they become more aware of their triggers - it will be second-nature.

When talking to your child, avoid asking leading questions such as, 'Are you nervous about the school play?' Instead ask open ended questions, such as, 'How do you feel about the school play today?' When children can start to put their own words to their experience and articulate how they're feeling, this helps them to engage their whole brain and process their experience.

Keep your tone of voice gentle when speaking to your child, and praise them when they manage a situation well, especially those that they find particularly stressful. It encourages them to engage in life and to let the anxiety take its natural course.

Take the fear factor away

It's crucial that children know that fear is natural and normal. You can take the 'fear factor' away, but don't remove them from the fear itself as this reinforces that there is something to be afraid of. My son, for example, is incredibly sensitive and lacks confidence. He loves riding his bike, even though he is frightened of falling off, so we took his bike to the park one day. As a result of focusing on his fear, he fell off his bike, cried and then got angry. I checked to see that he was ok, but I chose not to focus on his anger, or fuss too much over whether he was hurt. Instead, I said, 'Wow, what a good fall, we should have filmed that for your YouTube channel!' My son then laughed, agreed, then got straight back onto this bike. By focusing on his funny sense of humour and praising him for how well he was doing, this instantly shifted his mindset, as he was thinking about what was funny rather than feeling angry. Of course, he fell off his bike again, but realised he didn't hurt himself very much and that falling off his bike wasn't so bad after all! Instead of fearing what could happen and triggering his anxiety, he now had the experience to know that all would be okay, even if he did fall off.

Anxious children have a tendency to put pressure on themselves and will avoid things they find hard (the very things that lead to anxious thoughts), so praising them on their effort and progress instead of the end goal helps to build their courage and confidence. Through persistence and practice, children are stretching and creating new pathways in their brain. While something may feel hard, it will get easier, as my son discovered when riding his bike.

Introduce mindfulness techniques

Introduce and practice relaxation techniques when they are already calm. In time, they will be able to use them when they feel anxious. Bedtime is the perfect opportunity to introduce mindfulness but bear in mind that your child may take a while to adjust to the techniques. Anxious minds have a tendency not to switch off so even something like meditation can take a while to get used to. Experiment with some of the suggestions listed below until you find one or two that resonate with your child.

* Breath slowly and deeply through your nose while counting slowly to five for each breath. Exhale through your mouth. By breathing deeply and slowly, you slow down your heart

rate and restore your oxygen levels, reducing stress and inducing relaxation.

* Focus on your heart and tap your inner wrist in time with your heartbeat. You will notice it start to slow as you relax.

* Do something different to distract you and take your mind off your worries.

* Take some exercise; this releases the feel-good endorphins.

* Do something you enjoy doing.

* When your thoughts are distracting you, get present to your five senses: see 5 things, hear 4 things, touch 3 things, smell 2 things, and taste 1 thing.

* Talk about your child's favourite colour and how they feel when they see the colour, e.g. confident, happy, and self-assured etc. Tell them to see the colour in front of them, large and in 3D. Watch them smile!

* Hold onto something tight! When people feel that they're under pressure, they tense up physically. By squeezing on a ball or soft toy, for example, they can let go of their anxieties or stress.

* Think positive. Create some positive affirmations and mantras to repeat daily, e.g. I am loved, I listen to my heart,

I am safe. If you can get your child to do this in front of a mirror, even better!

* Listen to a guided meditation together or invest in some meditation-style flash cards to read to your child. This relaxes the body and mind and works brilliantly before bedtime, especially if your child has difficulty going to sleep.

* Listen to some music. If your child is more auditory, let them listen to some music to help calm and sooth.

* Read some children's books about worries and anxiety (there are a few recommended at the end of this chapter) or leave some lying around so that your child feels empowered to explore it for themselves.

* If your child has a tendency to worry at bedtime, ask them what their favourite thing was that happened in their day. This shifts their focus and fills their mind with happy thoughts as they drift off to sleep.

* Become a role model. Learn how to cope with your own anxieties. Children learn a lot from observation alone. How we handle our own problems can positively (or negatively) influence how they handle theirs.

How to Handle Meltdowns

Tantrums present a challenge for most parents, and they're not limited to toddlers (we have them too!). When your child is anxious, their meltdowns can become sporadic and unpredictable, regardless of their age. Living in a perpetual state of stress with hormones flooding their body means that they are overstimulated, overloaded, overwhelmed and have less control over their responses.

Quite often our child's tantrums can trigger an emotional response in us, particularly if we feel everyone is watching and judging our parenting. This can make us feel stressed and flustered and less able to handle the situation in a calm manner. Of course, there are times when children have very intentional and controlled meltdowns because they can't get their own way - don't we all have those moments? But an anxious child does not choose their tantrums; in those moments they are literally incapable of controlling their body or emotions.

As well as separate hemispheres, we can think of the brain as having an 'upstairs' and a 'downstairs', as coined by Dr Daniele J. Siegel and Dr Tina Payne Bryson in *The Whole-Brain Child*. The downstairs brain is the more primitive part and is where the amygdala resides, the component responsible for our innate reactions and impulses, and our strong emotions. The upstairs brain comprises the cerebral cortex - including the pre-frontal cortex, located behind your forehead - which controls our impulses, body and emotions. The pre-frontal cortex is the last part of the brain to develop fully; it doesn't reach maturity until we are in our late twenties. Because of this, children - in particular - tend to act before they think.

When the amygdala senses danger - which could be a genuine threat or a perceived one - the downstairs brain hijacks the upstairs brain; it takes full control. When a child has a meltdown - or 'flips their lid' - they're literally unable to act calmly and reasonably. The smallest of things can cause a child to become highly stressed because they don't have the words or ability to apply logic or reason to their experience.

As parents, we can fear 'indulging' or 'mollycoddling' our child's tantrums because we don't want to be seen as being permissive or raising a 'brat'. Quite often we'll resort to harsh responses or punishments in the hope that this will stop the behaviour. However, remaining calm and present to your child when they're flipping their lid isn't permissive, it's essential.

When our children are in the midst of a meltdown, they're unable to engage their upstairs brain. By helping to soothe your child and shift their attention, you can help them engage their upper brain and eventually calm down. Our goal isn't to reprimand our child but to help them calm their amygdala. In these situations, it's far more effective to use a more nurturing, loving and comforting approach to create connection with your child. As we've already established, anxiety is an extremely unsafe feeling. Responding to your child's emotional outbursts with high-emotion of your own - or even by ignoring them or pushing them away - can leave them feeling less safe and exacerbate their anxiety. Once your child has calmed down, only then can you respond with logic and reason and discuss the appropriateness or consequences of their behaviour.

It's imperative to remember that children are having their own unique experience, as we are, and that everything they think or feel is real, even if it looks different from our perspective. Empathy goes a long way, and if we want to raise empathic children, we need to model empathy in the way that we relate to their behaviour.

Recommended Resources:

Books:

'Hey, Warrior' by Karen Young
'The Huge Bag of Worries' by Virginia Ironside
'Little Meerkat's Big Panic' by Jane Evans
'The Whole-Brain Child' by Dr Daniele J. Siegel and Dr Tina Payne Bryson

"If you can dream it, then you can achieve it."

Zig Ziglar

Health and Nutrition

Are you struggling to keep anxiety at bay even though you meet regularly with a therapist, take your medication as prescribed, and have a reliable support system? The truth is, treatment for anxiety shouldn't stop when you leave your therapist's office, screw the lid back on the pill bottle, or step away from your family and friends—effective anxiety management involves one other significant factor: your diet. If you haven't tried tweaking what you eat, then you may be missing a valuable opportunity to beat back your anxiety.

There is a clear connection between the gut and the brain. Scientists and doctors now have a better understanding and continue to research this area. Adjusting your eating habits does not need to be daunting; small changes every day can significantly reduce anxiety symptoms.

Research shows that some foods act as natural remedies for anxiety, while others can send you into overdrive. Try incorporating these eight foods into your diet to reduce stress and anxiety:

1. Asparagus

Many studies going back to the 1960s indicate that many people who suffer from anxiety and depression have an elevated incident of folate deficiency. Asparagus is one vegetable that contains a valuable amount of this mood-boosting nutrient. One cup alone provides two-thirds of your daily recommended folate value.

2. Avocado

Vitamin B6 helps the body make several neurotransmitters, including serotonin, which influences mood. B vitamins - including thiamine, riboflavin, and niacin - have positive effects on the nervous system. Deficiencies of these vitamins have been linked to increased anxiety in some people. Avocados are rich in stress-relieving B vitamins and heart-healthy fat that may help to lessen anxiety.

3. Blueberries

When we're anxious and stressed, our bodies crave vitamin C to help repair and protect our cells, and blueberries are packed full of it. Small but mighty, blueberries are bursting with antioxidants and vitamin C which have been shown to provide anxiety relief. One study examined the effects of oral vitamin C supplements on anxiety in a group of students and found that antioxidants may be useful for both the prevention and reduction of anxiety.

4. Turkey

Ever heard of tryptophan? Tryptophan is an amino acid that the body needs to produce the neurotransmitter serotonin, which helps regulate sleep and mood. Tryptophan - found abundantly in turkey - has been shown to reduce anxious feelings.

5. Almonds

Researchers have shown that magnesium may be an effective treatment for anxiety-related symptoms, as low magnesium reduces the level of the neurotransmitter serotonin in the brain. Just 12 almonds contain 75mg of magnesium which is 19% of your daily recommended intake. You can also find magnesium in foods such as legumes, seeds, and avocado.

6. Yoghurt

Fermented food—including yoghurt —can help reduce anxiety! A link has been found between the consumption of fermented, probiotic foods and a reduction in social anxiety. The best yoghurts that contain 'live and active cultures' (such as plain Greek yoghurt) have 100 million probiotic cultures per gram or about 25 billion probiotic cultures in a cup. Other probiotic foods: pickles, sauerkraut, and miso.

7. Kale

Dark, leafy greens like kale, which is rich in beta-carotene and vitamin E, are needed to boost antioxidant levels and support optimal brain functioning to ease symptoms of anxiety.

8. Salmon

Omega-3 fatty acids - found in salmon - are particularly effective when it comes to foods that help with anxiety. Our brain requires the right dietary fats to function properly. Replacing red meat with seafood can ensure that we eat enough of the beneficial fats that support a healthy brain-gut microbiome.

People who suffer from anxiety should remember a few simple rules:

- Low blood sugar, inadequate hydration, alcohol, caffeine, and smoking can create, mimic or worsen symptoms of anxiety.
- Eat regular meals to preventing hypoglycaemic states (take extra note if you identify as getting hangry!)
- Drink at least six to eight glasses of water a day.
- Limit nicotine. People with anxiety may smoke to self-soothe, but nicotine raises blood pressure and heart rate and therefore increases feelings of anxiety.
- Reduce alcohol: excessive drinking can lead to its own set of emotional and physical problems.
- Limit caffeine, such as coffee and tea as they act as stimulants and can increase feelings of anxiety.
- Eat a well-balanced diet by reducing processed foods (e.g. packaged foods and takeaways) and focus on protein, e.g. chicken and eggs, that help you feel fuller for longer.

Sugar increases anxiety symptoms. There are many hidden sugars in the foods we eat, including savoury foods and those marketed as 'healthy' such as cereal bars and many types of yoghurt. Check your breakfast cereals and limit the number of condiments you have as things like ketchup are full of sugar. Many sugars are disguised with other names - such as sucrose, corn syrup, dextrose and barley malt - so you may find that your cupboards are full of foods containing multiple types of sugar.

While your body needs a healthy balance of sugar, carbohydrates, fats, and proteins to function, it is also that very balance that helps keep us healthy. Consuming sugar through natural sources such as a piece of fruit, and not fruit juice or dried fruit, affects your body differently than candy or hidden sugars in your foods. When fruit is blended rather than eaten whole, the sugar is absorbed into the bloodstream more rapidly. A study showed that blending apples and oranges yielded a glycaemic index 10-15% higher than what it would otherwise be if you simply ate the fruits whole. However, drinking a juice or a smoothie, for example, is still better than processed sugar.

It's always advisable to consult with your doctor before making any radical changes to your diet. I recommend seeking advice from a qualified nutritionist. As with any dietary change, your body will need some time to adjust so any benefits may not be felt straight away. If you are otherwise healthy and cut back on processed sugar, you may feel your anxiety slowly improve thanks to fewer ups and downs caused by the excess sugar and insulin spikes.

Exercise

Many people think that the mind and body are separate, but evidence actually shows that there is a link between being physically active and enjoying positive mental wellbeing. Furthermore, evidence shows that being physically active can protect people against depression and anxiety as it causes chemical changes in the brain which can positively alter mood. It also brings about a sense of higher self-esteem & self-control.

In addition to improved physical fitness, some of the mental benefits of physical exercise include:

- Less tension, stress and mental fatigue
- A natural energy boost
- Improved sleep
- A sense of achievement
- Focus in life and motivation
- Less anger or frustration
- A healthy appetite
- A better social life
- Having fun!

Adults are recommended to do 150 minutes of moderate activity every week, an average of 30 minutes five times a week. Even if exercising is challenging due to time and health, taking a brisk walk can help clear your mind and relax. I have had my puppy pug for 5-months now and have seen a massive improvement in my wellbeing. Having a dog benefits both you and the pet!

Exercising releases hormones that make us feel happy and help us sleep better. When you exercise, your brain releases endorphins, adrenaline, serotonin and dopamine. These chemicals all work together to make you feel good.

Below are some suggestions to help you become more active:

At home:

- Walk the children or grandchildren to school, then jog home.
- Speed up the housework. Tidy up faster until you feel warm.
- Put some music on for a 10-minute dance.
- Put more effort into all physical activity.
- Try an exercise app. Start at a gentle pace and increase as you feel your fitness improve.

At work:

- Time your daily walks to and from the train station or car park. Can you walk faster?
- If you work at a desk all day, google some desk exercises. Make sure you get up and move your body - even if only to grab some water - at least every half hour.
- Use the stairs instead of the lift where possible.
- Use your lunch hour to take a brisk walk, do an exercise class or go for a swim. Even if you don't exercise, use it as an opportunity to sit outside and reap the benefits of nature and fresh air!
- Don't pick up the phone; walk to see a colleague.

Out and about:

- Leave the car at home for short journeys.
- Get off the bus a stop earlier or get on a stop later.
- Walk the dog more often.
- Join an exercise class.
- Find an app on your phone such as the couch to 5k and find an accountability buddy.

- Even a short burst of 10 minutes' brisk walking increases our mental alertness, energy and positive mood.

Exercising has a positive impact on mood. It is low cost and helps decrease anxiety and stress levels.

Figure 7.1: Happy Hormones

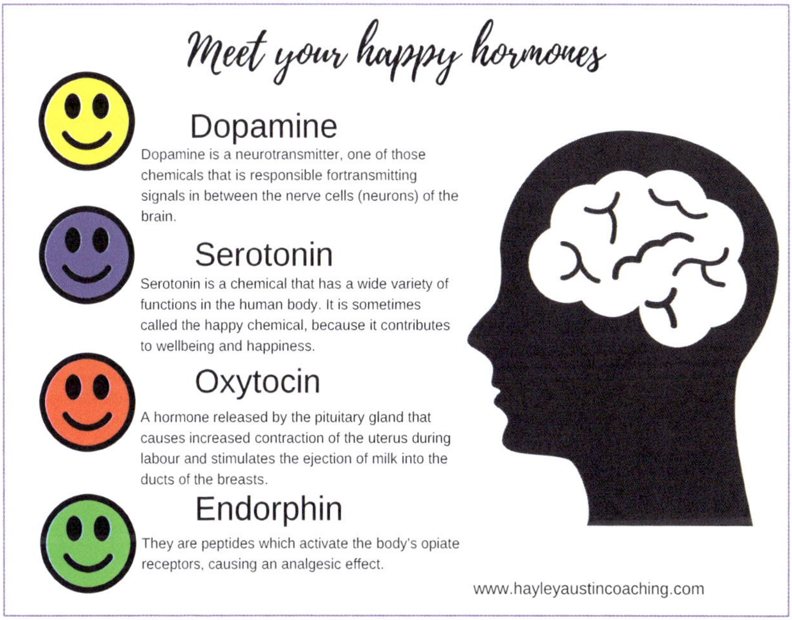

Keeping a Food and Mood Diary

Food diaries are useful tools to help us become aware of how certain foods and drinks - or even the times of day that we consume them - affect our wellbeing. I strongly suggest keeping one to track your daily progress and manage symptoms of stress and anxiety. You can keep a log in your regular diary or buy a specific food diary online from places like Amazon. There are also some great apps available too including the Cara: Food, Mood, Poop Tracker.

While you can try to keep track of that information in your mind, it's so easy to forget what we have consumed. All too commonly we over-consume or under-consume, and rarely attribute any symptoms that arise throughout the day to what we've eaten. Putting your eating and drinking habits in writing can be pretty eye-opening and bring awareness to some of the underlying factors contributing to your symptoms and overall wellbeing. It's useful to know which foods are impacting you physically, mentally and emotionally so that you can avoid them. Equally, it's helpful to know which foods lift your mood and energy.

It's imperative when keeping a food and mood diary not to judge or shame yourself. Be totally honest about everything you consume without attaching any guilt to your eating and drinking habits and review your diary objectively. The more we bring our habits into our awareness without judgement - no matter how negative or destructive we perceive them to be - the better placed we are to do something about them; sticking our head in the sand does not create positive action!

Figure 7.2: Example of a Food and Mood Diary

Breakfast	**Breakfast**
mood	mood
Snack	**Snack**
mood	mood
Lunch	**Lunch**
mood	mood
Snack	**Snack**
mood	mood
Dinner	**Dinner**
mood	mood
Snack	**Snack**
mood	mood

As well as noting your mood, hunger and bowel movements, write down everything you put in your mouth – liquids, gum, candy, medication, and supplements, as well as food. Note the time of day that you consume something and list a general description, e.g. white/brown bread, white/brown rice.

The Psychology of Your Health Habits

Of course, much of what has been covered in this chapter may prove futile if you don't address the deeper issues: what is driving your eating and drinking habits? We have more access to science and research than ever before; we know what is good for us. Yet, we still consistently choose to eat the foods that cause us pain, drink the alcohol that triggers our inner demons, and avoid exercise even when our increasing weight is causing discomfort.

When we have a low sense of worth, it's hard to muster the motivation to do what is needed to effect change. Equally, poor self-esteem and a need for external validation may lead to obsessive health habits such as 'clean eating' addiction or compulsive exercise.

As we've established in this book, much of our behaviour is driven by the memories, beliefs and experiences stored within our unconscious mind. When we bring them into our conscious awareness and release them using NLP techniques – or other modalities such as hypnosis or life coaching – our 'bad' habits fall away, creating space for new behaviours to emerge.

If you know that you need to address your diet and exercise, go back and work your way through the exercises in this book, focusing specifically on these areas.

Epilogue

All the answers you need are already within you; you just need a little help to find them from time to time. This book has given you tools, tips and strategies to do just that so you can take back control of yourself, your health, and your life.

Anxiety can be crippling, but it doesn't have to limit the quality of your life. Whenever you start to feel yourself wobble and those first fleeting feelings creeping back, pick up this book. Use it as part of your regular maintenance, so those attacks become less frequent. It's so easy to think that we're cured and then become complacent, ending up back where we started; I don't want this for you.

I want this guide to be your travel partner, your confidant, your friend, to be dipped into as and when the need arises. And most of all I want you to know that, no matter what, you can be happy, healthy and in control, in spite of what your anxiety tries to tell you.

About the Author

Hayley Austin is a Life Transformation Coach and uses NLP (neuro-linguistic programming), Talking therapies and Clinical Hypnotherapy to help people become the best version of themselves, with particular focus on those who are stuck or stressed. Hayley coaches people locally and has also developed an online coaching business to reach out and help more people with anxiety, stress, fear, and confidence.

Before becoming a coach, Hayley spent 6 years building her Network Marketing business, leading and growing an award-winning team. Before becoming an Entrepreneur, Hayley worked all over the world from Morocco to China managing and developing operations in the commercial imports/exports industry. After the birth of Hayley's son in 2012, her values changed, and she discovered NLP and life coaching. Hayley now helps many people - from executives to stay-at-home mums - find their true purpose and takes clients on a unique journey to build a rewarding future.

Hayley is currently studying a masters in NLP, Hypnotherapy and Life Coaching as well as being a tutor for the UK Life Practice academy in Hitchin. She has won awards for her coaching and prides herself on being an empath to give her client's the most powerful and life-changing coaching experience.

Hayley lives in West Yorkshire with her son Jacob, a puppy pug called Polo, and her husband Mark. She enjoys learning new skills, thrives on personal development, loves walks by the sea, prosecco, spending time with her family, holidays - and shopping!

Hayley is available for speaking events, marketing and projects, as well as private consultations.

Visit her website to download her free resources, including meditations and workbooks.

Connect with Hayley:

Email: hello@hayleyaustincoaching.com

Website: www.hayleyaustincoaching.com

Facebook: www.facebook.com/hayleyaustincoaching/

Twitter: @hayleylifecoach

Instagram: www.instagram.com/hayleylifecoach/

LinkedIn: www.linkedin.com/in/hayleylifecoach/

Acknowledgements

I would like to express my special thanks of gratitude to my coach Mark Shields.

My journey of self-discovery began in August 2017. I felt like there was a part of me missing and I couldn't quite put my finger on it. I wasn't living my purpose, and I felt I was living my life for other people and meeting their expectations. Now my life has changed on what I can only describe as a massive scale. A complete Life Transformation! Mark Shields - CEO of Life Practice UK - is my mentor and coach. Through him I became an NLP Practitioner, Clinical Hypnotherapist and Talking Therapist; he taught me everything I know. Mark encouraged me to become my true authentic self, to embrace my gift of empathy towards others, and to use it to help empower many people to become the best version of themselves. Mrs Powers was born, and my Life Coaching journey began with my eyes wide open. Mark teaches you to 'be the difference that makes a difference,' and I really feel that now I am making a difference. I will be forever grateful to Mark and everything he has taught me.

I would also like to thank Michelle Catanach for helping me write this book. I had so much I wanted to include in the book that I had already written, and Michelle brought my project together. Thank you, Michelle, for your support and assistance.

I would also like to thank a local charity for their partnership. I worked with so many men and women, all with unique stories. It was a great honour to be part of their journey to recovery and a better, brighter future, full of opportunity.

Printed in Poland
by Amazon Fulfillment
Poland Sp. z o.o., Wrocław

56855522R00123